THE
NIGHTINGALE

SAM LEE

CENTURY

Dedicated to Oran Summer Cecilia Lee
and to all those who stop to listen.

1 3 5 7 9 10 8 6 4 2

Century
20 Vauxhall Bridge Road
London SW1V 2SA

Century is part of the Penguin Random House group of companies whose
addresses can be found at global.penguinrandomhouse.com

Penguin
Random House
UK

Copyright @ Sam Lee

First published in the United Kingdom by Century in 2020

www.penguin.co.uk

A CIP catalogue record for this book is available from the British Library.

ISBN 9781529124835

Printed and bound in Italy by L.E.G.O. S.p.A.

Penguin Random House is committed to a sustainable future for our business,
our readers and our planet. This book is made from Forest Stewardship
Council® certified paper.

MIX
Paper from
responsible sources
FSC® C018179

CONTENTS

INTRODUCTION

It was twelve long months since first we met
So early in the spring
When the small birds they did whistle and
The nightingales they sang.

'The Tan Yard Side', traditional English
folk song, as sung by Phoebe Smith

According to folk song, birds merely whistle, but the nightingale sings. How can it be that this little brown bird, in so many ways indistinct from his fellow scrub-and sky-dwelling companions, has risen to a status vocally so far above the accolades for any other bird?

Before we embark on the wondrous journey concerning how this bird has sung his way into so many worlds, lives, languages and laments, I should add the caveat that the nightingale is, in every respect, rivalled by many other technically gifted and virtuosic species. The crooning wailings of the curlew, the incandescence of the blackbird, the declarative whoops and hollering of the song thrush or the travelogue retellings of the marsh warbler singing back the fragments of other birds heard on its migration – these songs all warrant the same level of human adoration and reverence, but somehow nightingales got the fat worm, when it came to notoriety and cultural elevation. This comes down to timing – not just the spacious, rhythmic patter and patterns in their song, but their chosen time: the night-time. When most other creatures rescind their notes, leaving the land a darkened theatre between performances, in comes the nightingale, putting on a springtime show.

Every bird tells a story, and each of these stories tells something of that feathered kind and of their weavings within the tapestry of our human world. Like a prism splitting light-beams, the nightingale and his song refract localised notions of place, home, matters of the heart and rootedness. Though weighing in at only a few grams, the migratory nightingale carries enormous symbolic and sentimental gravitas in all of its summering homes, and appears on the tongues of people in varied levels of localised esteem, through legends, tales and songs, each one imbuing our bird with greater depth and nuance. In sub-Saharan Africa, where the nightingale winters, there seem to be few cultural references to the bird, perhaps because it does very little singing at this point in its life; but nightingales reverberate across Europe, the Caucasus, the Near and Middle East and all the way over to the Indian subcontinent, in some of the oldest music known to humankind. Nightingales are master infiltrators, finding their way into secular folk song and sacred devotional music alike.

I came to meet the nightingale through folk song, the ancient, anonymously scribed repertoire native to the British Isles that often traces itself outwards to lands far away. Folk songs describe the various interplays between humans and the landscape. They nod to the ways in which we encountered the land, its flora and fauna – including, of course, birds. I have always been a child of nature, spending my youth and early adulthood studying the arts of nature connection and wilderness bushcraft skills with masters such as Ray Mears and Jon Young. In my early adulthood the discovery of folk song was like finding a lost hieroglyphic, a language of connectedness and enchantment sparking an exciting, deep love and hunger for these songs to be learned and sung.

The anthropologist in me, however, needed more than manuscripts and recordings to satisfy this new-found thirst and, aged twenty-five, I embarked on a journey into song-collecting. I set out to try and source the last singers stewarded in an unbroken line of oral tradition across the UK and Ireland. What I found would change my life. Like discovering a meadow of thought-to-be-extinct flowers that is soon to be ploughed over, I met the last of the Gypsy Traveller 'source singers': aged members of the community who, in their lifetimes, had witnessed the final days of a nomadic, itinerant way of life, brought up in tents and caravans with lives lived as close to nature as can be. Many still held the great wisdom of plant-lore and had an unbelievable awareness and magic-knowing of the land and what lived upon it (creatures recognised, but sometimes from the realm of the unknown). Their songs were perquisites of this gathering of old lore, and often in their recounting I met the nightingale. I recorded as many of these elders as I could, drinking down the songs before the well ran dry, as it has almost done today, because most of these song-carriers have now passed on.

But the songs live on, even if the old keepers don't; and as Gustav Mahler testifies, 'tradition is tending the flame and not worshiping the ashes'. My duty is to find those flickering flames and feed them with the most organic nutrients possible; to find the 'fat of the land', rendering it down as new fuel to light new fires. Nightingales are a flame so widely depicted and referred to that their notoriety would appear to be inextinguishable. However, with their numbers rapidly depleting in England today, the reality is very different. Numerically speaking, their flame is reduced to the fragility of a lit matchstick leaning towards an oncoming gale. They are a litmus paper to the land, and a barometer of all beings.

And it appears that throughout the ages this luminescence has always been the nightingale's role, in prose and poetry as well as folk song. The nightingale's beak has been the nib through which many emotional evocations have been penned. Nightingales have carried down the ages their own repertory of associations – starting, as far as we know, with the ancient Greek poets and philosophers, appearing in medieval epics and then in the romantic woes of the British literary giants like Keats and Clare. Each spokesperson was tutored and informed by the associations of this bird in worlds past, and by the local folkloric appreciations prevalent at that time and in that place. In the voices of the people, unpublished folk songs internationally sing of the many characters that the nightingale holds, clothed in an ambiguity of posturings. We find the nightingale singing in sorrow, in sexual pursuit and in duplicity; in lament, in playful rejoicing and even in wise consultation; but it is always a bird rich in – and a conduit for the many names of – love. The nightingale comes to us today with a wealthy inheritance, and its treasury increases with each era.

You'll hear of my initial encounter with a nightingale in the first chapter of this book. But circumstances forged me to this bird in a way I could not have expected, or wish would ever have been. On that first trip in search of a nightingale, my party included a heavily pregnant friend, Polly Renton, an inspiring documentary film-maker, ethical journalist and mother of four-year-old Rosita. After our initiation, experiencing for the first time the nightingale's darkened realm and his night-song, we retired to our tents. There, huddled together, I sang a favourite folk song of mine, 'The Tan Yard Side', as quoted above, opening with the lines 'I thought she was an angel bright, come tripping down so low'. It was only hours later that Polly went into labour with little Tristan. At the end of May the following year, Polly and Rosita were both tragically killed in a car accident near their home in Kenya – Tristan miraculously surviving. My usherettes to the nightingales had vanished, to become the angels in this song. And ever since, when hearing these birds sing on their spring return, I hear the voices of Polly and 'Sita still shining 'like diamonds bright', their spirit fused within these tiny song-carriers. Such is nature's power to acquire and hold the memory of the emotional turmoil we live through and, in turn, to offer healing and guidance to reckon with the challenges we are dealt.

The nightingale applied a similar balm to the nation in 1924 via the seminal live radio broadcasts pioneered by Beatrice Harrison and the BBC, which instigated a national outpouring of appreciation for this bird. It took on a new modern role in an electrified society, which preceded the beginning of the bird's population decline after the Second World War. In the BBC's broadcast that I made to celebrate Beatrice's work on the ninetieth anniversary of the original airing, I stepped away from being just a listener to being, like Beatrice, a nightingale collaborator.

The programme led me to establish my 'Singing with Nightingale' concert series, which provides others with the opportunity to hear the birds in correspondence with human musicians. In turn, that has led me on a journey of learning about the healing power of nature and the nightingale's role, as I see it, as 'head surgeon' in this practice. During the months spent gathered with human friends and strangers, the nightingales have become my confidants and teachers, and have offered for many people an intimacy with nature that is so necessary in the nature-deprived lives we now lead.

To know the name of a creature is not enough to know who it is, and I could never claim that this book will contain everything that has ever been known about the nightingale. It is in no way a definitive biography – not even a brush with the wings of this bird – for its world is so huge and the stories connected to it are so many. Instead, this is a preliminary introduction to the nightingale's biological and anthropogenic appearances; the chapters that follow are some of the significant strands in the web of its many worlds. Their niche is small, but it is pitted within; and through our own gaping dents on this Earth we reveal many of our beautiful (as well as sometimes brutal) legacies. These niches shift and shape according to our own lightness and shadow: some glorious, others shameful; some greedy, violent and exploitative, and others generous, spiritual and deeply beautiful. The nightingale has perched himself above us as night-watchman, singing back to us his own testament to our doings. The following chapters are just some of his many accounts.

My thanks go to all those who have guided me to this bird and helped deepen my understanding and expand the nightingale's mystery. Special thanks go to the Renton Family, Nick Lear, Tom Stuart for his exceptional knowledge and brilliant ears, the RSPB's Adrian Thomas,

David Rothenberg, Becky Burchell, Rachel Millward, Tiff Wear and New Networks for Nature. But especially to Oran Summer, my daughter, who – aged three months when first taken to find nightingales – managed to bring a male right up to us, which sang all over us in full sight, something I never imagined I'd witness. Thanks also to all those who have dared to join my reckless journeys in the dark, torch-free, and have revealed how important it is for us to hear and protect the nightingale's song.

CHAPTER ONE

DECORATOR OF SILENCE: FIRST ENCOUNTERS WITH THE MASTER SONGBIRD

There are only a few 'first times' in our lives that we would ever retell with such unbridled wonder as our first meeting with a nightingale. You might have 'held hands' with nature many times, but hearing the song of this bird is a rite of passage, akin to your first kiss. Perhaps your meeting was by day, or maybe you disobeyed reasonable behaviour to embark on a night visit when you would usually be returning home. Maybe you haven't met one yet; maybe you will soon.

My first meeting with a nightingale still seems like an unworldly baptism, a nocturnal awakening and a revelation that nature had fully arrived, filled with artful compulsion. I've long believed that the natural world's glorious treasures appear in ways that only nature herself decides, and not always in the dependable, convenient way we hope to experience them, on our terms and to our time-keeping. As the rule goes, when out seeking enchantment on nature's ground: never expect. The whimsical – even capricious – way nature offers up her rare gifts means that you often have to make great preparations to experience those delicate encounters, or be lucky enough to be in that special place at that special time. My first nightingale moment was pure luck. This tiny bird led me across a threshold and introduced me to a way of being in nature that I'd never reckoned with. The experience was a meditation on stillness, yet also a provocation to dance with abandon.

In not such a dissimilar way to birdsong, at the heart of the folk-song tradition – for which I am an interpreter and arranger – lies the solo unaccompanied voice. Silence is a vital part of the composition of performing in that old way. This bird singing unadorned in the raptured quiet of the night, so similar to my core practice when performing without any instrumentation, challenged me. The nightingale exemplified the daring possibilities that many artists aspire to. This was a guide to musicality; a masterclass in melodic explorations. In the nightingale,

I had finally found my teacher and guide to instruct me in the great art of decorating silence.

It was after dark on a mid-May evening at Arlington Reservoir in Sussex and my friends had invited me to hear the nightingale sing. The night was chilly, as the day's heat had condensed into a heavy dew, so I was wrapped up warmly, in readiness for my quest to find a bird that I'd never thought of seeking out, let alone making a pilgrimage to find. I've never considered myself a birder watcher twitcher. I wasn't even sure what these terms really meant. I had worked in bushcraft when I was younger, so I have always been close to birds. But the nightingale is not a bird that can readily be seen in parks, gardens or in most parts of the country. An encounter with it requires planning.

That night my friends and I reached the edge of the reservoir, with its tall, woody treeline in front of us. In the distance I could hear the unusual drips and diphthongs – gliding vowels – of something that, at first, didn't seem bird-like at all. The sound seemed too sinewy, too muscular even, to come from a bird. In the disorientation of the night I began to doubt my own ears. I even questioned whether one of my friends was taking me for a ride. But as we approached, the sounds grew in resolution, became cleaner and more fulsome.

We wandered, uncertain, towards the source, stopping and reorienting ourselves as the sounds grew closer and closer. The air felt heavy with the nightingale's song, in the same way that the smell of a hawthorn hedge-line in flower, with its sweet, fetid scent, lingers in the nostrils. The nightingale's song induced a similar response, an intoxicating, sedating sensation. The birds seemed to breathe a musical condensation that dripped from the branches of the trees in inky deliquescence.

We sat and listened to the nightingale's aria for what felt like hours. Other nightingales rose up in response, and a polyphony of birds emerged, weaving the woods together. To me, the song was visual, despite the darkness. The night was pitch-dark and silent, and my eyes filled in the black with sonograms that vibrated, grew and resonated with the waves of music, producing a bodily synaesthesia in this sleeping wilderness. I was reduced, childlike, to a state of wonderment, grinning inanely and transported through deep time, deep song and deep earth.

After this first night-time liaison, I became obsessed by the thought of hearing the nightingale again and learning more about this elusive bird, whose name preceded him (and it is a *him*; the female nightingale will rarely be heard to sing, except occasionally, right at the end of the season). That mystical, breathtaking song comes from the male of the 'common nightingale', perhaps the most notable of the night-singing birds.

Of course the nightingale is not the only night-singing bird, and only sings for a few short weeks each spring. But the male nightingale has definitely taken the lead actor's role in the theatre of the night. At this hour he is not in competition with any other birds. His fellow companions – owls and nightjars, maybe a dunnock or a cuckoo – will spark up, but there is no other bird that sings so continuously and so unabated through the night and then into the daytime. The nightingale deserves our commendation for sheer commitment to his art.

Knowing the nightingale

The nightingale, a nondescript little brown bird, so plain and yet so elegant, disguises his genius well. Both male and female birds sport a warm-brown rump and tail with a grey-brown underside. Their throat is a dusty chalk-white, as if they have brushed past the white cliffs of England's coast on arriving home. In his seminal title *The Birds of the*

British Isles, published in 1925, T. A. Coward describes the nightingale as 'a large, handsome brown robin'.

Unlike robins, nightingales are not easy to spot, even when their song seems to be right next to you. Their movement is often described as 'skulking'; this is a bird that prefers not to be seen. Some of you may have had the good fortune to hear a nightingale, but have you ever seen one? If so, you are in the minority. Most people have to work very hard to find them, so secretive is this bird. It took many years of listening before I actually found myself in the sightline of one. If you do catch the nightingale in song, you'll notice how much energy is invested in this expression, throwing his head around and bulging his throat like an opera singer.

Key characteristics

The common nightingale is related to the redstarts and wheatears that occasionally grace British shores and belong to the 'chat' family. The chats, in turn, are classified within the order of Passeriformes (commonly known as 'passerines'), along with about half the world's bird population. Passerines are 'perching birds', but are more usually known as songbirds. Their most common feature is their feet: three toes face forward and one backwards, enabling them to balance steadily on branches. The passerine order also includes birds that are not thought of as songbirds, such as bowerbirds, corvuses (crows) and even herons.

Measurements

Length: 15–17 cm
Wingspan: 23–6 cm
Weight: 17–24 grams

redstart

robin

thrush nightingale

Appearance

Feathers: Brown above, with a reddish tail; buff-white below

Legs: Pink

Beak: Blackish-brown, thin, medium-length, with a golden-yellow mouth and throat

Natural habitats: Woodland, wetland and grassland

Notes: Nightingales look similar to robins, but are slightly larger and do not share their red breasts. In flight, redstarts, which have paler red tails with a dark centre, are often confused with nightingales. The common nightingale should not be mistaken for the thrush nightingale, which visits parts of Europe but not the UK. These two birds look very similar, and the best way to differentiate them is by comparing their song. The tonality of sound is similar, but the thrush nightingale doesn't display anywhere near the bold decadence of his common cousin. As the name suggests, the thrush nightingale's song is far more repetitive, displaying the thrice-repeated phrase rhythm of the song thrush.

Migratory birds

Roughly sixteen million birds form the 'Great arrival' to the UK each spring and summer, equating to approximately a quarter of our total bird population. Several billion more birds flock to the central and southern European countries, plus north-western Africa, and over to western Mongolia in similar latitudes. The current migratory routes are believed to have remained consistent since the end of the last Ice Age, about 18,000 years ago. When the lands thawed, the birds ventured north, as habitats flourished and warmer fertile lands emerged from the post-glacial wastelands.

As soon as the nightingales arrive in the spring, the song commences. The males are thought to arrive in their familiar territories slightly ahead of the females, ardent and ready to attract the hen nightingales flying overhead. At the end of the breeding season, from mid-August until the beginning of September, the call back to their antipodal home comes, as autumn approaches and the temperature begins to drop. Travelling at night to benefit from the cooler temperatures and to avoid predators, the nightingales undertake the treacherous 6,000-km return journey south. Their fuel reserves and stamina are tested as they make their way across the English Channel into northern France,

The Nightingale's
migration route

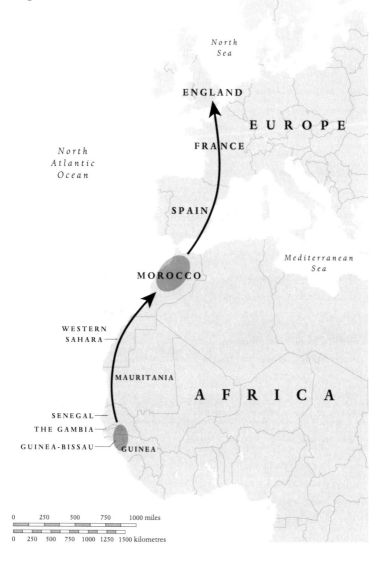

down through Spain and the coast of Portugal, often aiming for the Strait of Gibraltar to cross over into northern Africa. Most birds will pause somewhere before northern Africa to refuel and lay down more body fat, ahead of the toughest part of their journey.

The passage of the British nightingales then takes them around the west coast of Africa, although some birds embark on the hazardous route directly across the Sahara. They will rest when they reach the scrub of the West African sub-Saharan areas, such as Sierra Leone, Senegal and Guinea-Bissau, and then spread themselves across several hundred square kilometres of land. Here they will circulate from country to country, capitalising on abundant food sources and warm weather until it is time to set off on the long journey north again, around February or March.

The British Trust for Ornithology (BTO) has been working to track and monitor nightingales over the past few years, with the development of light micro-transmitters. In 2009 a nightingale tagged in May in Methwold Hythe, on the edge of the Norfolk Fens, was recorded in the north of France at the end of July and in southern France by mid-August. At the end of August and into mid-September he was located in northern Morocco, before crossing the Sahara, with a possible stopover in the Western Sahara. He spent his winter in Senegal and Guinea-Bissau.

The Pfeilstorch

Strangely, bird migration wasn't truly understood until relatively recently. It was once thought that the swifts that disappeared as winter approached were hibernating in the mud at the bottom of a lake; that birds transformed into other creatures; or even that they flew all the way to the moon. The first confirmation of the migratory journey came in May 1822 in Mecklenburg, Germany, when Count Christian Ludwig von Bothmer captured a stork that was roosting on his chimney. Lodged through the bird's neck was a hunting spear and, looking at this spear, the count realised that it appeared to be of African origin. Later research identified it as belonging to a sub-Saharan African tribe, and it became clear that this migratory bird had flown all the way from Africa, bearing the weapon of some hungry hunter. This original *Pfeilstorch* (arrow stork) was later stuffed and is now on display at Rostock University in Germany – the first of numerous *Pfeilstörche* that have since been sighted across Europe, after narrow escapes with hunters.

Home

The word 'nightingale' stems from its habit of night-singing: *gale* for 'songstress' in its Germanic roots. In Europe it is also the *nattergal* (Danish), the *Nachtigall* (German) and the *näktergal* (Swedish). In its species name – *Luscinia megarhynchos* – *Luscinia* comes from the Latin *luctus*, meaning 'lamentation'; *megarhynchos* is from the ancient-Greek *megas*, meaning 'great', and *rhunkhos*, meaning 'bill'.

Biogeographically speaking, nightingales are Afro-Palearctic, meaning that they breed in the lower latitudes of Europe, across into western Asia and then, like many of our migrant birds, winter in Africa. Their most westerly point is the south-east of England, although some venture just over the Devon–Somerset border. Kent, Suffolk, Essex and Sussex host the majority of the 5,500 estimated English singing males; their numbers have thinned out elsewhere in the country. In other parts of Europe their population is more robust; about five million pairs breed on the mainland. In northern Europe and Scandinavia the thrush nightingale (*Luscinia luscinia*) adorns the night with its beautiful, if somewhat less elegant, song, and the two birds overlap through Germany, Poland and Romania.

There are no formally recorded incidences of the nightingale reaching Ireland or Scotland (though the Irish call the blackcap the 'Irish' or 'March nightingale', and the sedge warbler is often identified as the 'Scottish' or 'Irish nightingale'; both have beautiful songs). While there has been the occasional report of a nightingale crossing the Offa's Dyke boundary, Wales does not host the bird, although the Welsh name *eos* is perhaps the finest of all the other native names for our bird.

Might there be a coincidence in this distribution – often described as comprising an area roughly below an imaginary line between the Severn estuary and the Humber – approximating to the limits of the last glacial maximum? Probably not, but I like the idea that our birds hold an epigenetic memory of where that wall of ice once ended, knowing never to venture further, and heeding an ancient warning of what once was.

So, is the nightingale an English bird? Nightingales are born in England, summer in England and are associated with the English pastoral.

Nightingale distribution
in the UK

Shetland
Islands

SCOTLAND

*Atlantic
Ocean*

*North
Sea*

**NORTHERN
IRELAND**

*Irish
Sea*

IRELAND

ENGLAND

WALES

*Celtic
Sea*

*English
Channel*

| 0 | 50 | 100 | 150 | 200 miles |

| 0 | 50 | 100 | 150 | 200 | 250 | 300 kilometres |

Shakespeare and Keats wrote about them as one of their own (more on that later, see page 172). I like to think, though, that the nightingale symbolises worldliness and has a global character, an intercontinentality. In some ways the nightingale song has a wildness that is in disaccord with the traditionally perceived modesty of the English countryside. Perhaps it is the influence of the sub-Saharan forest habitat, in which nightingales spend so much time. No doubt they experience a whole other sonic world when they winter in Africa, where they must find a different soundscape – a sound-environment of non-European animals, birds and invertebrate brethren that populate the forests and savannah scrub. But then so do many of our other migratory birds that share these same wintering grounds. Yet the nightingale also mirrors a stereotypical Englishness in its shyness, politeness and inventiveness. So many personalities emanate from this near-invisible creature.

Courtship

Nightingales return to breed in their summering grounds each year, coming back to almost exactly the same place they left, usually within 200 metres of the nest they were born in. Their homing memory is incredible, using a combination of 'true navigation', which requires landmarks to navigate, the sun's 'compass', and detection of magnetic fields. This homing ability is not fully understood, and is even more impressive considering that their first journey to and from sub-Saharan Africa is mostly travelled at night and alone (nightingales don't travel in 'flocks', like many migrating birds). It's only in their summer habitat that nightingales maintain fidelity to one spot – that is, with a nesting site they come back to when they, hopefully, return to breed the following year. Unfortunately, in the UK their population is declining year-on-year, and soon they may no longer call this island their home at all. The nightingale is on the UK's Red List of Threatened Species, which details those at greatest danger of becoming extinct here.

The nesting territory is selected by the male nightingale, which usually returns to the same area as the previous year. The birds are hugely fussy about where they live, which is one reason why reintroducing them, or trying to maintain a habitat specifically for them, is difficult.

The females, or hens, will often seek a mate in a different region from previous years, giving them the best chance of finding the right mate. They move around in the first hours of nocturnal nightingale song, listening, and if they hear a male that interests them, they come down. Then, in the daylight, they will inspect the territory for a day or so, to see if it's up to scratch. A courtship dance may occur – with softer singing and fanning of the tail by the male, or gentle pursuit in flight.

The cock nightingales aim to mate within six weeks of starting their song. Once the courtship has finished, the hen builds a nest low to the ground; or even on the ground itself, within the leaf litter, hoping that the dense scrub and thick coppice will form a barrier against dangers both above and around. The nest is sometimes described as messy and loose, with an outer layer of leaves and a softer lining of moss and grasses, hair and other fine filaments. There the nightingales stay until, around mid-May, the hen lays a clutch of pale-green eggs, usually four or five. She then sits on them for about twelve days before they hatch. Both parents take responsibility for feeding the nestlings for the two weeks until they are able to fly, and then usually for a little longer after fledging.

In mainland Europe the length of the season allows for two broods, so the males will sing all summer; but in the UK the cock stops singing once the young have hatched. Nightingales school their young with rather more garish calls and cries, their sublime recital having finished for the year.

Only about half the male nightingales succeed in securing a mate each year. The rest will sing on till late May, their song becoming weaker and appearing later at night, until they give up on a partner for that year. I like to think they sing out still for the sheer joy of it, while they can. Most birds only live for a year, and nightingales rarely live longer than two – the general toll for a migratory songbird. For some males, their song is their true moment of glory.

How the nightingale got his song

There is an old story ... It begins long ago in the big forest, when the whole world was one great wood: tree after tree after tree. It had come to that time of year when the birds felt a pull of the plumage, a ruffle in the down and a twitch in the tail feather – that urge to find a mate. But as all birds at that time were brown and feathered, with not a speck of shade or colour, the issue arose of how to differentiate one species from another. It was the source of much confusion.

So a conference was called, and the Council of Birds gathered together to discuss what could be done to rectify the situation. All night they nattered, until each species had been heard and all ideas explored. But, alas, they couldn't reach a decision they all agreed upon. It was beyond their powers, and they concluded that a higher help was required – this was a question for God.

So a date was set for them to make a visit skywards and give their request. On that day, representatives from each of the forest's bird species flocked to the highest point of the highest tree on the highest hill, alighting on that top twig and flying upwards. Higher and higher they went until they reached the first nimbus cloud, floating gently overhead. They entered the damp mistiness of the enormous cloud, then continued flying higher and higher still. Eventually, bursting above the clouds into the higher atmosphere, they flew onwards until they reached the high trade winds and wispy cirrus clouds. The birds beat their wings harder, battling against the thin air and the cold, which was particularly biting for the smaller birds. Larger-bodied birds like geese gave the finches a piggyback, while wrens rode on the back of eagles, hummingbirds on herons. It was a collaborative effort and no one was left behind. Finally all the birds arrived into that uppermost layer, a liminal space between Earth and the heavens that we have no name for. And there lived God.

They went up to the front door of God and knocked loudly. Instantly the door opened and there she stood expectantly. 'Come in, birds,' she beckoned. So one by one all the birds entered God's beautiful home and presented her with their quandary.

God thought it over for a short while, and then a smile crossed her face. 'I think I may have a solution for you all. Come with me.'

And so the birds followed her into her workshop. And out of her cupboard God pulled a big box of paints. Opening the box, she took out all the tubes and paintbrushes. One by one, she called the birds forward to give their feathered plumage a fresh painting: the robin, his beautiful red breast; the blue tit, his Titian-blue feathers; and the kingfisher, who was a very expensive bird to paint. Each bird was given a new set of markings and, after a few moments to let the paint dry, leapt with great joy off the front porch of God's home and flew back down to the forest.

All except for the nightingale, for he – being a very shy bird – was too nervous to step forward to make his demand. By the time he'd plucked up the courage to step up to God and say, 'Please could I have some colour?', she thought her work done and had run out of paint. He pleaded with her, asking if there was something left in her tubes for him: 'Just a dab? Anything? I don't mind what colour.'

God looked through her paints, peering down each tube, and by luck found one with a speck of something left in it. So she took her most special paintbrush – the one with a single hair on it, plucked from the whiskers of a nightjar (with his consent) – and pushed it deep down into the tube of paint and swirled. As she took it out she said, 'Nightingale, I can't make you much to look at, but I have an idea … Open your beak.'

And so he opened his beak as wide as he could, and she gently placed the paintbrush down his throat and dropped the little fleck of shining golden paint.

'Nightingale, I'm giving you a golden voice,' she said.

Nightingale was rather pleased with this. With a big smile, he leapt off her doorstep and glided back down to Earth.

Through the whippings of the trade winds he flew, but he was much later to leave than the other birds. Dusk had arrived, and the beginnings of an enormous thundercloud rose from below, sucking him into a mighty thermal column. Nightingale was caught in the most almighty gusts of wind and found himself being tossed round and round. Breezes of hot, moist air took hold of him and then hailstones flurried past, pummelling him. Warm currents pulled him upwards, then cold ones thrust him back down. Lightning and thunder sparked all around him, and all of a sudden he was gripped in an icy downdraught, covering him in frosted crystals. He was spat out at the bottom of the thundercloud and dropped down to Earth.

There he landed on a mossy patch of his very own forest, exhausted, but – luckily – unharmed. He picked himself up and shook his feathers down. Realising where he was, nightingale flew immediately back to his wooded patch.

By this time, night had come, and we all know what happened at night in those days: there was a great cacophony, and this night especially so. Every bird in the forest sang wildly. It was utter chaos, and a deafening noise. You couldn't hear a thing. It was just a blast: all the different notes, and all the birds discussing their plumage and what they had seen on their journey. Nightingale, happy to be home and ready to join in, flew to his sounding post and opened his mouth. To everyone's amazement, out came the sweetest song anyone had ever heard. As his notes travelled, one by one the birds in the forest fell silent in awe, listening to nightingale and his new song.

The very next day the Council of Birds was called once more to discuss nightingale and what to do. They couldn't just sing over such a beautiful song. It was decided that nightingale was to be given the night to himself and, come the evening, all the birds would fall silent. And so it is that, to this day, nightingale is still the holder of the night. Occasionally he'll allow some of his ensemble to join in, like the owl and the nightjar and a few others; sometimes a dunnock. And still, to this day, nightingale is an exceptionally shy bird. If you ever manage to get a peek at one, you'll notice his lighter bleached front, from his throat down to his belly button, from the harsh ice crystals he flew through. And if you get yourself into exactly the right position and look down nightingale's throat as he's singing, you'll see the sparkle of gold still there to this day. And that is how the nightingale got his song.

J. Roller sc.

CHAPTER TWO

THE WOODS: HABITATS AND HUMANS

The woods and birdsong go hand-in-hand in a far more prosaic way than first meets the ear. Fire has been central to our existence for hundreds of thousands of years, and has been part of our culture and language and mythology. Fire is the forest's latent carbon storage transformed into pure energy: the tree is sacrificed to sustain our ever-evolving habits and habitats.

This primal fire has been a hungry child in all communities, and copious amounts of fuel had to be gathered constantly to sate its appetite. Before electricity, the places we inhabited needed to be as close as possible to a ready supply of coppiced or timber-producing woodland.

As society and habitations flourished, so we developed our skilled trades, crafts and infrastructure, and people acquired an ever more sophisticated need for woods of varied species, different ages, lengths, grains and properties. This was a time when every implement, tool, mode of transport, weapon and home was made from wood, or from metals that needed smelting through the thermal properties of wood or charcoal. The cooking we did, the baking and brick-firing, the drying of harvests and the general convocations of people – all demanded heat. This was powered in turn by woods, which were our power stations and fuel cells.

It goes without saying that habitations across the West depended on the woods. Imagine a landscape covered with deep temperate and well-stewarded woodlands, from which humans naturally sourced material in a way that we would now trumpet as 'sustainably harvested'. Maintaining enough wood without clear cutting (clearing an entire forest back to the ground) meant long-term thinking, and working with the pace of the slowest-growing trees.

The common practice of silviculture – managing the growth of woodlands and forests – across much of the deciduous woods of

Europe, in order to keep a continuous and renewable source of wood, was coppicing. Using this practice, trees are cut back to their stumps in winter to harvest the wood and, come spring, allow young shoots to grow an indefinite supply of future poles. The root systems of the new growth are established, providing quicker regrowth. Neolithic wooden trackways uncovered on the Somerset Levels have shown coppicing's long use, with hundreds of equally cut coppiced poles laid as a rudimentary trackway. The major benefit of coppicing for local ecosystems was the prolific diversity of plant and insect life, sustained by the increased light and water available to the ground from opening up the canopy. After a few years the dense regrowth becomes a prolific habitat, abundant in thick vegetation, invertebrates and, of course, birds.

The nightingale thrives in this man-made tree garden, finding it a superb ecological niche and a habitat perfect for its choosy homemaking. Through this ability to regenerate our trees – which, according to George Monbiot in his book *Feral*, evolved in response to the destructive behaviour of pre-glacial megafauna, such as mammoths and woolly rhinos, as they browsed and uprooted their way through those early woods – the nightingale came into close contact with the humans exploiting this trait for their fiery needs. So right from the original times of slashing and burning, humans have inadvertently nurtured the nightingale's habitat and, year in, year out, over those spring months have spent a glorious six weeks listening to the nightingale on his return.

Years ago, the mixed agriculture landscape in the UK would have looked markedly different – large hedgerows and deep dykes were created as ways of partitioning fields and holding livestock. That pastoral system would have been the perfect environment for the nightingale, with the thick, messy margins between fields. But misfortune struck the bird during the Second World War, when the 'Dig for Victory' campaign commenced a steady and gradual pilfering of those habitats, and so their decline began. So much semi-arable land, scrub and woodland was cut down to make way for agriculture; agricultural policies encouraged the removal of hedgerows to maximise the productivity of land; and people were incentivised to dig up scrubland. Most farms also had scrapes (wetland areas) or small ponds that were enormous wildlife havens, but in the 1970s the government paid farmers to fill them in and thus increase the farmable area. All these changes in land stewardship had removed prime nightingale areas. And now another home for these birds, the dense scrub of willow and blackthorn that grew around a pond or boggy area in a field, was suddenly removed. Little by little, we destroyed the nightingale's habitat and, in doing so, we began to lose their song.

Nightingales nest low to the ground – they need cover from above. In the coppiced landscape they appreciate the three-to-five-year growth. This can come from a mixture of woods, ranging from sweet chestnut, birch, willow and hazel to the classic English staple of hornbeam. After a few years the coppice reaches a prolific density, which, along with a profusion of undergrowth reaching up in the newly provided light, creates an almost impenetrable habitat. This furnishes a highly safe understorey for feeding, which enables the bird to source its food by exploring and pecking around during the day looking for ants, beetles, worms, ground larvae, spiders and small invertebrates among the leaf litter.

This aspect of coppiced woods only lasts for a few years, though. Once the stems grow too high and leggy, the dense canopy shades out the ground layers, emptying the thick growth and creating a more open – and thus less nightingale-friendly – habitat. The bird would be forced out of the coppice, were it not for the foresters, bodgers and woodworkers cutting sections of woodland in rotation (rotational cop-picing), which supports the nightingale when one area grows out, as another area close by reaches a state of favourability.

Coppicing is the human-manufactured environment that is prefer-able to nightingales, but they also haunt dense scrubby areas. These principally hawthorn (mayflower), blackthorn, willow, bramble or wild-rose environments grow up as thick blisters of green in the land-scape. Again, such thickets are profuse and biodiverse pockets of flora and fauna. Growing to about 4–5 metres high, these coverts look like bubbles of brambles with a mass of vegetation, which protects the in-sides of that wild green knot from browsing animals.

Such thickets provide a shell over the nightingales' habitat – a green leafy barnacle on the grassland. If you took a cross-section, you would see that it is completely hollow inside, with bare, leggy branches creating an open space for birds to nest safely in the low levels and forage down below. The thorny bramble jacket makes it difficult for predatory stoats, weasels and squirrels to get in and steal eggs, or for greedy ravens, crows, rooks, magpies or jays to savage the nest. This external protection is well noted by nightingales when choosing a nest-ing site.

In Africa, the bird sees a completely different landscape. There's no courtship during the 'winter' and no eggs to protect, so there is no need to build a nest. Instead, nightingales move around woodland and scrub frequently, and are able to be more mobile and responsive to their en-vironment, flying large distances sometimes to different territories, as and when food becomes available as the season progresses. Their pri-ority during their wintering period is feeding, in preparation for their return home. Studies in Tanzania of the thrush nightingale, however, have shown that males do practise new songs while wintering.

UK decline

In England, the males are so fixed to their home areas that the habitat crisis hits them hard. Their level of expansion and movement is small, so particular are they. Not a lot is known about their movements, and only now are we starting to learn details of their behaviour at home and abroad. But despite enormous efforts to create ideal habitats for them in the UK, we are still seeing a population decline in places where we would have hoped for an increase.

The drop in nightingale numbers in Britain is a consequence of many different factors. The loss of habitat brings with it a reduction of adequate food sources, and this has to be a major cause. The survival rate confirms that the birds are not able to raise enough offspring or breed offspring strong enough to survive the journey back to Africa. Depleted habitats are not as flush with insect life as in the past, and nightingales are losing the competition with other birds and species for the nutritional gains they need. A cataclysmic concoction of climate change and temperature, an imbalance of species and the crash in insect life, due to farming practices and the overuse of insecticides, has devastated their particular food sources.

One of the largest factors that experts consider to have aggravated the effects of climate change are the ballooning populations of muntjacs or 'barking deer' (you may have heard them barking loudly, like wild dogs, at night). Muntjacs are a very small Indian deer, introduced in Bedfordshire early in the twentieth century and now widespread across England. Low-down browsers, they like chewing and ripping away areas that are sensitive to protecting the nightingale habitat and producing the food sources for insect life. Deer populations in general across the UK are out of control, with no predators left, and humans are uninterested in eating them in large enough quantities to make a difference. Deer have become one of the major contributors to habitat destruction, fatally ring-barking trees (stripping the bark in a ring from the tree's circumference), devastating unprotected ancient coppice stools by eating new shoots, and browsing so much lower-level vegetation, which thins out the density of scrub and bush.

There is such a complex series of balances and cause-and-effect ensuing in the English countryside right now, and some birds are surviving well in these environments and don't appear to be suffering the same rate of decline. Perhaps it is the nightingale's particular sensitivity, and its inability to find the right habitat to roost, that has affected its breeding. However, the 2019 UK *State of Nature* report, combining the research of seventy wildlife organisations, assessed there to be a '13% decline in average abundance across wildlife studied and that the declines continue unabated'.

We also have to consider the global issues of the nightingale's wintering time. It could be that they are not surviving the flight from Africa because the intensification of agriculture and farming practices there are shrinking habitats and are preventing them from feeding adequately over the winter to endure the journey back. The declining availability of insects means less body fat to propel the birds northwards, and they are exhausted before the journey's end.

The British Trust for Ornithology is responsible for much research into nightingale territories and breeding trends, and its model for climate change suggested a likely increase in nightingale territory, and that – like other species, such as the Dartford warbler – the nightingale's habitat would move further north with the warming temperatures. Alas, this has not been the case and its English territory is still shrinking south-eastwards; the reasons for this are still not understood, and it indicates a far more complicated set of requirements that the nightingale depends on for its survival.

Resisting extinction

I head to the south of England to hear the nightingale sing every year at the same tantalising moment that spring is firmly stirring from its winter sleep. The surge of anticipation at being received in the woods by the birds is palpable, like standing at a train station awaiting the arrival of a dear old friend.

On 19 April 2019 the nightingale's return came at an incredibly poignant time. The first of my annual public nightingale-visits coincided with a global awakening to the ecological and climate emergency affecting all species, including the nightingale. The climax of the civil disobedience led by Extinction Rebellion (XR) took place in central London. At the heart of this protest was a stranded pink boat emblazoned with the words 'Tell the Truth', which was beached in the middle of Oxford Street. People from all walks of life came together to display acts of resistance, love and solidarity. For many of us, this radical consolidation was filled with extraordinary displays of creativity and defiance, from civilians and celebrities alike. At the peak of these surreal and world-changing ten days, Dame Emma Thompson climbed aboard the yacht, reciting words that echo inside me to this day: 'Dear Earth, I couldn't live without you.' Had I not had guests waiting for me in the field, I would have stayed; but the nightingales had arrived just the night before, and we had a date to honour. I detached myself from the picket lines and fled London as the full force of governmental power was thrown at quelling this brave display of defiance in defence of our fellow species.

Leaving the hard streets of London for the woods, I went from one act of protest to another. My undoubtedly romantic and whimsical annual nightingale-pilgrimages – taking audiences and musicians into the woods to improvise and sing with the birds – was, I realised, a protest in itself. Like XR's radical reclaiming of London, I took to the woods to rebel at the silencing, and at the inaction to our environmental crisis on our own doorstep. Through song, through campfires, through stories, through just turning up and declaring my love for this tiny creature, I was leading my own small rebellion.

As I led my first group through the darkness to hear the song, I approached the nightingale's habitat that year with trepidation. This Kentish population lives within woods protected with the absurdly named but vital protective status of 'Site of Special Scientific Interest' (SSSI) – as if only scientists would find it interesting. On this opening night, the trees were electrified with multiple nightingales singing to each other after a year of separation. As we grew closer, my eyes began to puddle. These tears of grief could only be released once I had fully detached myself from the love and rage that a week of protest had opened within me.

I felt as if I were being reunited with an indigenous tribe in full ceremony, rich in language, customs and kinships; but I came with the knowledge that this world might be too cruel and too complacent to permit their existence to continue. I listened to these nightingales, as our ancestors had done for millennia, but heard them now with a whole new appreciation. I began to hear the birds, so often associated with broken hearts and forlorn lovers, singing of the sadness of their extinction.

The nightingale's song of rebirth had become a requiem and I acknowledged, for the first time, that in my lifetime I will see these birds extinguished from our land. Within thirty years nightingales will be silenced in the UK – erased, existing only in memory – their loss a testament to our neglect. If they go, then eventually so will we. That night their song was more radiant than I'd ever heard it before.

CHAPTER THREE

SONG SEEKERS: HOW TO FIND A NIGHTINGALE

People often ask me, 'How do I find a nightingale?' Despite their dwindling numbers, however, nightingales are easy to find, if you want to. When I dig deeper behind the question, I often uncover a lot more about our relationship with the natural world, exposing a combination of uncertainties and rifts that have grown up between us and nature, as the unknown. What if I can't find one? Isn't it dangerous being out in the woods late at night? What if I look stupid in the woods in the dark? Can I get lost? What if I get cold or it's wet? What if I disturb the nightingale? How will I recognise his song? Where will I park? Who would possibly go with me and not laugh at me for suggesting such an idea? What if I fail? What if nightingales are better in books and poems, and folk songs, than in real life?

These are all, of course, good questions and speak so much of the myriad fears that many of us have about entering nature, especially at night. Perhaps I don't give enough credit to those who dare themselves to go out into the woods after dark. Maybe you consider yourself a hardened rambler, right-to-roamer or intrepid explorer – such confidence is a great privilege. For many people, the local heath, park or marsh on a sunny day provides all the nature they need. Taking to a cold, wet, dark forest after sunset is akin to a heated-indoor-pool swimmer swan-diving into a winter Atlantic swell for a hearty wild swim.

For the majority of us, realising the sense of permission to access nature has been highly eroded, and in few places in Europe more so than in the UK. Our list-topping rate of nature depletion in Britain is a testament to, and utterly entwined in, that worrying decline. This individual sense of permission is also radically different, depending on your socio-economic situation; even more so if you are Black, Asian or of any ethnic minority. There is an irony to this, especially as what we have in the nightingale is the poster bird for a global citizen, and the vision of a borderless passage for a migrant. As a musician who regularly encounters visa restrictions, I think upon our bird in this way with envy.

First, though, you have to find your singers – and below is a list of sites where I have come across nightingales singing within the last four years. This list is by no means comprehensive. Nightingales live in many more places, but this represents a healthy selection of sites under the stewardship of the Woodland Trust, the National Trust, the RSPB, the Wildlife Trust, Natural England, NGOs and other such bodies that have good access rights.

Finding a nightingale is not always easy on a large reserve or site, so prior research will help your journey. Many people do this via social media or Internet searches. Birders often post about sightings on Twitter, so in just a quick Internet search and a few clicks you might find where they are. Enthusiastic birders or NGOs' social-media teams will often offer fast and enthusiastic responses, with location details, if you message to ask them. This flow of information is given out generously, but be mindful of whether or not the bird is on publicly accessible land or private property. Please also be aware of any stipulations about the site's code of conduct. Always be especially conscious about dogs in bird-nesting sites in spring, and enter any such habitats as respectfully as possible, to create as little impact as you can at this sensitive time of year.

Stepping into the night

Before you go to find a nightingale, my advice is to ask yourself before leaving, 'Does my bum sound big in this?' Your experience of listening to the bird is utterly dependent on how noisy you are on your expedition. The old saying goes, 'There's no such thing as bad weather, just unsuitable clothing.' In my experience there is a scale of inverse proportion: the more you spend on a high-tech weatherproof garment, the brighter and louder it is ... Journeying into the outdoors to open up your senses and drink in the sounds of nature is completely undone if you're wearing a 'crisp packet' jacket, as I call it. In the stillness of the night, all you can hear is the swish of your arms or your waterproof trousers, letting everything out there know you have arrived, and giving it a chance to scarper before you had any idea it was nearby. Such garments completely consume the sound-world around you and render you unable to hear anything that is moving, singing, alighting from a tree, hooting or barking.

Call me old-fashioned, but the solution lies in one word: wool! It has all the properties you need for walks out in the cold and dark. It's completely silent, super-warm and when wool gets wet, it can absorb enormous amounts of water without feeling damp. It's also very hard to find good woollen outdoor wear in bright neons. You are therefore spared a glow-in-the-dark presence and can start to play with the 'invisible', which is important when looking for nightingales.

So it's early May, you have committed to the adventure, are all wrapped up and have made it to a site where there are nightingales. Unless there's a bright full moon, you're likely to encounter something we hardly ever get to experience these days: true pitch-black. Your eyes have probably encountered artificial light en route, and your pupils will be dilated accordingly. The intention of the journey is, of course, to hear nightingales, but it also serves to deepen and open your sensory perception. In meeting them, you can in some ways *become* them. Follow their example and let your senses accommodate the ambience of the woods, acclimatising to the darkness and silence. How much you want to dare in this playful inhabitation is up to you. Either way, you will experience a sensory shift in the dark, a handover of leadership from your eyes to your ears, skin and nose.

You probably have a strong torch, a phone for showing your GPS and are wearing heavy walking boots. This would seem an obvious kit list, but it isn't as fail-safe as it sounds. Torches are a double-edged sword: they illuminate what is in front of you but, in doing so, they send your peripheral vision into a relative blackout. This comes with many compromises. At night our eyes adjust to a very different style of seeing. The human eye's retina depends on photoreceptive 'rods' and colour-sensitive 'cones'. In the dark, the rods focus our capability on seeing movement detail over colours. We lose the acuity of our central vision, and thus rely more on our peripheral vision. Torches create an extreme tunnel vision, which is actually more likely to disorientate us. Night vision takes nearly twenty minutes to build to full strength, so a torch can quickly undermine all of that work.

If you must use a torch, try to find one with a red-beam function, or mute the beam with your fingers, so as to let out only a sliver of light: just enough to guide you, but allowing a full 360-degree awareness, which brings the stars into view and provides depth of sight into the near-distance. Always keep the beam to the floor and never point it at anything, especially the nightingale. Likewise, put phones away and don't be tempted to look at them. If needs must, put your phone under a sleeve and read it through the fabric, to dull the intensity.

If you like a challenge, I put this invitation out there to you: switch off all your devices, put away your torch and take off your shoes and socks, then proceed barefoot into the territory of the nightingale. Your soles – one of the most sensitive parts of your body – are almost always bound up in impenetrable shoes and denied any sensation, so the impact on your body of walking barefoot into a wood will be mind-blowing. The activation on your pressure points gives you the most electrifying experience. It will change the way you move and hold your body, and will create an almost *Alice in Wonderland*-form of bodily transformation.

Look at any medieval tapestries and see how the soft-bound feet of figures seem to have pointed toes. In societies that didn't have hard soles as standard, and when journeys were often across infirm paths, we would walk toe-to-heel, touching the ground with our toes first and then falling back onto our heels, taking our body weight down with them. In this way we first tested the ground for stability, sharp objects, holes and humps. We nimbly navigated our way with a far more engaged gait, which reduced the impact and shockwaves that today cause many ankle, knee, hip and back complaints. We were never meant to walk straight-legged on hard, flat surfaces, which rarely occur in nature. Watch how a child bounds across a meadow and instinctively places his or her feet as just described.

Notes on silence

The intention is to stay playful and enter the theatre of this exercise as though it is a performance. Don't be fooled by the still quiet of the night-time woods. Everything is firmly aware and listening, so by staying in character you tell all around you that you are part of the performance and not blundering across the stage, despite them. You are stalking this nightingale, not maliciously, but with respect.

Before you embark on your expedition, make sure you know what the nightingale song sounds like! Taking moments to pause and listen deeply is so important for locating your nightingale. Use the 'owl ears' technique to seek out distant sounds, by cupping your hands behind your earlobes. Using subtle movements and adjustments, you can focus your ears' reach hundreds of metres further than normal. At regular intervals slowly scan the landscape for any bird calls or night-sounds. Stillness in the body is vital. We are usually deaf to the noise we make, but the amount of sound that we emit from our breathing, rubbing of clothes and shuffling is extraordinary.

When not listening deeply, breathe deeply instead. I like to breathe in through my nose and mouth together, in order to fully smell and taste the air. In spring you can pick up the aromatics of budding, blooming or bruised plants and, with some training, our noses can divine further ahead than our eyes and ears. A fox's skunky spray or some wilting garlic ransoms, the fetid stench of mayflower, the vanilla drops of a poplar tree, the rain on soil or stones are just some of my favourite early-spring smells. There is so much to discern in the air that can tell you about what is around you, even when you can't see it.

When you have located your nightingale, move nearer. The males usually choose high perches to sing from, so you can get exceedingly close and, as I say, 'look right up the skirt of the bird'. The rest of the experience is up to you. I always sit and listen to his song first, before offering into the space some overtone throat harmonics – Mongolian-style throat singing. The high harmonic whistles, in the same pitch as the bird's song, seem to really stimulate the nightingales, which immediately connect with this ancient Eastern style of singing. Maybe this book can provide inspiration for other things to offer, but finding an experience that feels pertinent to you, and your world, is the most important thing. Enjoy!

Where to find the nightingale

Every nightingale habitat is different, and each site presents different obstacles and access problems. In some places it is easy to get close, and in others the birds are far off, deep in a dense, impenetrable thicket. That uncertainty is all part of the joy and challenge of seeking them. In my by-no-means-comprehensive travels to find nightingales in the UK, I have experienced their company in many wonderful places, but my favourite five sites to hear them are as follows:

Fingringhoe Wick, Essex

Essex Wildlife Trust looks after Fingringhoe Wick, which is one of the UK's finest nature reserves. In high season it simply drips with nightingales, and the overgrown reclaimed gravel pits buzz like a rainforest with their song. This is a portrait of what our country must have sounded like not many years ago.

Green Farm, Shadoxhurst Woods, Kent

Green Farm is situated by a large stretch of ancient woodland leading out to Romney Marsh, and the SSSI has a growing population of birds in amongst some privately owned but easily accessible coppiced woods – a successful example of collaboratively cared-for privately owned woods.

Knepp Rewilding Estate, West Sussex

Knepp Estate is similar, and you can read more about it later in the book (see page 210).

Snape Maltings, Alborough, Suffolk

Snape Maltings is the majestic classical-music centre that grew out of Benjamin Britten's 1948 Aldeburgh Festival. The converted malthouses now form a campus of venues and music studios, nestled in the watery reedbeds and marshes at the mouth of the River Alde. This Area of Outstanding Natural Beauty (AONB) hosts only a few nightingales, but the rich wetland environment means there are vast numbers of other species to tell a wonderfully bird-rich tale. I appreciate Snape enormously for its sensitive integration of a cultural hive within a thriving wetland ecology.

Other notable sites are:

Arlington Reservoir, East Sussex (South East Water)
Blakes Wood and Danbury Common, Essex (National Trust)
Cotswolds Water Park, Gloucestershire (CWP Trust)
Derring Woods, Kent (Woodland Trust)
Durford Wood, West Sussex (National Trust)
Grafham Water, Cambridgeshire (Anglian Water)
Hydon's Ball and Heath, Surrey (National Trust)
Martin Down Nature Reserve, Hampshire (Hampshire County Council)
Moat Wood, near Lewes, East Sussex (Woodland Trust)
Paxton Pits, Huntingdonshire (Huntingdonshire District Council)
Sutton Hoo, Suffolk (National Trust)
Swan Barn Farm and Bookham Commons, Surrey (National Trust)
Westleton Heath, Suffolk (Nature England)
Witley and Milford Commons, Surrey (National Trust)

The RSPB has previously noted nightingales at the following sites:

Blean Woods Nature Reserve, Kent

Cliffe Pools Nature Reserve, Kent

Highnam Woods Nature Reserve, Gloucestershire

Langford Lowfields Nature Reserve, Nottinghamshire

Minsmere Nature Reserve, Suffolk

Northward Hill Nature Reserve, Kent

North Warren Nature Reserve, Suffolk

Pulborough Brooks Nature Reserve, West Sussex

Snape Nature Reserve, Suffolk

Stour Estuary Nature Reserve, Essex

Wolves Wood Nature Reserve, Suffolk

Highnam Woods is a nightingale site worth singling out, given its tragic decline in nightingale numbers. I run the Gloucestershire 'Singing with Nightingales' visits here, and in 2017 they had twelve singing males. The following year there were six males, and in 2019 only three singing males were heard. Who knows what their future holds? The RSPB is doing a great deal to try and halt the losses and improve diversity, but numbers are still declining, despite huge investment in providing nightingale-friendly habitat.

Berlin, Germany

If you want to combine nightingale-listening with some contemporary culture, late-night techno clubs, Bauhaus architecture and high art, then Berlin is the place to go. The *Nachtigall* is in much more robust health at the heart of mainland Europe – even in a bustling metropolis like Berlin. Here there are about 1,500 breeding pairs in the city alone, in the city's parks (including the large Tiergarten right in the centre), in mature gardens, and in patches of green.

In Berlin, Sarah Darwin (the great-great-granddaughter of Charles Darwin) is leading a team providing the research that informs nightingale students around the globe. Darwin and her team have created a huge amount of interest around the nightingale's song, alongside the composer and ornithologist David Rothenberg, who leads regular musical collaborations with the birds for the public in the Tiergarten, as well as at Treptower Park. I will never forget coming offstage one April in 2016 after a concert at the Haus der Kulturen der Welt, situated in the Tiergarten, and taking some air in the back garden, which stands between the concert hall and the Bundeskanzleramt. Suddenly a nightingale shot up, singing, right in front of me. I was blown away that in this urban complex, just metres away from Angela Merkel's desk, I was listening to this rare but familiar song.

To the woods

The British Trust for Ornithology (BTO) has a fantastic track record in monitoring species spread and decline, and in research into the likely causes, such as habitat destruction and predators. It conducted a survey in 2012 to track nesting nightingales across the south of England. Allowing for birds that were probably not located, it came to a figure of 5,542 territorial males in the UK, of which 70 per cent were to be found in Suffolk, Kent, Essex and Sussex. Even in these densely nightingale-populated areas, there is still a measurable decline. The BTO website and its BirdTrack portal form a brilliant asset in searching out locations of all bird species, not just nightingales. For detailed and up-to-date sightings, this is an invaluable resource for seeking places to hear nightingales.

These are all the tools you need to find a nightingale. The incentive and nudge to step up to this challenge, and go and find a singing bird, are now up to you. At the end of this book I propose a conceit to enact your own 'occasion' – one that I call a 'Nightingaler' (see page 212). This book and all its gathered resources, stories, songs and prose to come would reach their fullest realisation, were they to be your companion on such a journey.

Philomela luscinia. Linn.

Cromol. G.Bressler. Milano.

CHAPTER FOUR

THE LADY OF THE NIGHTINGALES: BEATRICE HARRISON AND THE BBC

Almost every country that hosts the bird has its unique associations with the nightingale, be that its cultural and/or musical repertoire or its traditional stories with the bird at the centre. There seem to be endless ways in which this bird is framed within myriad cultural expressions. The UK has its own nightingale 'origin story' that is still told today – a story that brought the nightingale deeper into our consciousness (and households) than ever before. It may not be a connection steeped in ancient history, but this event and the particular nightingale involved could, in many ways, be considered the first-ever viral media sensation ...

A remarkable family

At almost every nightingale event I attend or host, someone will ask me if I've heard of 'the woman who played with nightingales'. That woman is Beatrice Harrison, and as well as being one of the most legendary British cellists, she is responsible for changing my relationship with this bird and, in doing so, changing my life.

Beatrice Harrison was a true notable of the early twentieth century. A renowned virtuoso cellist, a vibrant and charismatic woman, she was born in India in 1892, the second of four daughters. Music was always going to play a major part in their lives. Their mother, a talented singer, took a grand piano over to India when she moved out there with Beatrice's father, who was serving in the Anglo-Indian army. Many hours were spent singing and playing to, and with, her young children. Beatrice's older sister, May, could apparently sing before she could talk and was a gifted pianist by the age of three, then took up the violin. The younger sisters, Monica and Margaret, were also singular musicians from a young age. Beatrice took up the cello when she was eight, before she was even as tall as the instrument itself. Three years later she and May won scholarships to the Royal College of Music in London.

Beatrice's wonderful autobiography, *The Cello and the Nightingales*, tells how they would spend hours practising each day under the tutelage of a range of visiting piano and string teachers. Once the sisters had learned all they could in London, the Harrisons divided the family. Beatrice and her mother moved to Germany, so that Beatrice could study with the distinguished cellist Hugo Becker, while May went to St Petersburg for further violin schooling. Beatrice's public debut came in 1910 when she played Brahms's Double Concerto for cello and violin with her sister in Berlin.

Both sisters won awards and accolades for their performances on the continent, and tours of Europe, Russia and America followed. Over the following years the sisters acquired a long list of admirers and friends, among whom were many composers, conductors and musical names of the day. Beatrice was a darling of the classical music scene and her career blossomed, and composers of the time seemed to be queuing up to work with her and dedicate their music to her (her most notable partnerships were with two of the biggest names of the time, Edward Elgar and Frederick Delius).

Royal connections

By all accounts, Beatrice was a lively character – she loved dancing and the theatre, and life was filled with plenty of social occasions. This was an era when women weren't as free to enjoy such independence, but Beatrice and her sisters made up for that inequality in their spirit. Beatrice was often seen, and heard, playing within the high-society circles of the time. On being invited to play at the home of Lord Crewe, on the occasion of a visit from King Edward VII and Queen Alexandra, she began a close friendship with their daughter, Princess Victoria, which was to last her entire life.

When not indulging in bohemian night-time balls, Beatrice – and indeed the whole family – was devoted to their menagerie of animals. On their return to London from Germany, she listed their returning cargo as including 'at least 50 canaries, all the lizards and fish, the snakes and the tortoises'. Beatrice would claim that her 'greatest love was birds. We had about 50 canaries, many of which we bred ourselves ... What I loved best was to hear the Master Canary teach his sons to sing.'

The garden

After years of worldly travels and a debonair lifestyle, the beginnings of a new partnership were to begin back in Beatrice's country home. In 1923 the family moved to Oxted in Surrey, to a 'cottage' called Foyle Riding. The grounds were significant – Beatrice talks of them having six gardeners – and the following spring the gardens were 'declared glorious', helped by a meadow of blue flowers, from seeds royally gifted from the greenhouses at Sandringham. Beatrice describes one particular evening as being 'so lush' that she ventured into the woods adjoining the gardens and sat down to play some of her favourite pieces on her cello. In a moment of silence a sudden burst of birdsong, in imitation of the cello's notes, exploded above her. She played on and, much to her surprise, so did her accompanist. She was entranced.

'I used to wonder about the garden, you know, with the cello at night. It was always a joy to me. And one night, when I had been playing for hours, I suddenly heard the note of the most heavenly bird. Of course I'd never heard the nightingale. But the next day, our dear old gardener came along in such excitement. "Oh," he said, "the nightingale's come back again. I believe it's the cello." He used to sing in thirds with me and it was such a joy. He used to twiddle about – well, he was always in tune with the cello.'

The next year Beatrice's career reached new heights when she performed the first radio broadcast of Elgar's Cello Concerto. There was a growing awareness of technology's potential to share music with millions of listeners, and her entrepreneurial mind wandered towards her nightingale, which had returned that year to her Oxted garden.

After the transmission she spoke to the announcer, Rex Palmer ('Uncle Rex'), and raved about 'her' bird – and her desire for others to hear him. Rex didn't seem to think this was impossible. And so, enthused by his blessing, Beatrice telephoned Lord Reith, then Controller of the British Broadcasting Company, to ask the team to come and record her nightingale. The fledgling BBC had been formed just two years earlier, and Lord Reith, much to Beatrice's surprise, turned up his nose at the idea, unsure if this was really what the public wanted to hear. He must have considered the expense of the project and deemed it a waste of BBC resources. But Beatrice was insistent. It was mid-May, and she knew that her nightingale would be singing later and later each evening and would shortly fall silent. The race against the season was on.

At the same time BBC engineers, pioneers in the burgeoning radio industry, saw the unique opportunity and supported Beatrice's idea. With new media technology still evolving, the capability for outdoor broadcast had yet to be tested anywhere in the world. This seemed like an exciting, if somewhat unconventional, prospect for the BBC: it had never before broadcast live from outdoors, never mind live birdsong. A test run was signed off by Lord Reith, and the date was set for 19 May 1924 – late in the season, but not impossibly so.

On 18 May a party tripped down to Foyle Riding to test the grounds, led by Captain Peter Eckersley, the BBC's first Chief Engineer. In that initial test broadcast they relied upon the newly purpose-built Marconi-Sykes magnetophone, which was far more sensitive than previous technology. It was positioned underneath a tree, with about ten accumulators providing the power, some batteries and a great deal of cable. Nearby, in a thatched summerhouse, they positioned the large amplifier, which would magnify the signal to be sent down the wire. There are myths about what happened next. One story is that the engineers unwound miles of cable, tracked the massive battery packs and equipment through Beatrice's garden and waited, only for the bird to stay silent.

Whether true or not, the sensitive microphone certainly picked up signals the following night. At first, unidentified sounds were heard, later attributed to squirrels and rabbits nibbling the wires, with the odd

rhythmic insect whirr. They waited for the nightingale to sing, but it was silent. For a long time no bird was heard. A no-doubt-tense Beatrice remembered the crucial moment: 'Suddenly, at about quarter to eleven on the night of 19 May 1924, the nightingale burst into song as I continued to play ... I think he liked [Rimsky-Korsakov's] "Chant Hindou" best for he blended with it so perfectly.'

Rex Palmer was the announcer that night, as he had been just days earlier for Beatrice's Elgar Cello Concerto. Reports say that he broke into transmission of the Saturday-evening performance of the dance band, the Savoy Orpheans, and announced a sudden change to the schedule. Alas, no recordings of that initial broadcast exist, but we do have later broadcasts to suggest what was heard: the scratchy fragments of Beatrice playing Dvořák, Elgar and the Londonderry Air (more commonly known as 'Danny Boy'), along with the elegant and intricate voice of the nightingale.

Consider how unusual it must have sounded for listeners to be thrust suddenly from the concert hall into the woods, listening to just a solo cello and a bird singing. Compared to the boundary-defying programming that we tune into today, this would have been utterly radical radio broadcasting, and a novel experience for listeners.

A phenomenon

Despite the many potential technical issues, the duet warbled its way down Foyle Riding's telephone line to 2LO, the central-London BBC transmitter. It then took flight skywards to homes across the land, and indeed across the world. And the world *was* listening. That late-night duet elicited a phenomenal public reaction. It was reportedly heard by around one million people across the globe, and it is claimed that those without radio sets phoned friends who had them and listened to Beatrice and her partner down the earpiece.

The *Daily Sketch* recorded the moment: 'with astonishing clearness, the liquid notes of a nightingale singing in the Surrey woods at Oxted were heard by many thousands over the wireless last night'. A reported 50,000 letters were written to Beatrice afterwards, some addressed simply to 'The Lady of the Nightingales'.

The new microphone technology permitted an unprecedented auditory clarity, which helped spark such a powerful emotional connection to the nightingale. Perhaps the song tapped into a collective memory of those raised on the land, possibly even near nightingales, but now transposed into urban centres and an aspirational metropolitan existence. The visceral burst of 'woman with nature' into so many homes (and remember that radio was still new, and television as yet inconceivable) was remarkable. This was a cultural moment not dissimilar to the moon landing forty-five years later, which made listeners stop and think about the changing world and what they had left behind.

Lord Reith's review of the programme made the front page of the *Radio Times* on 6 June. He said that the nightingale 'has swept the country ... with a wave of something closely akin to emotionalism, and a glamour of romance has flashed across the prosaic round of many a life'. He later added, 'Milton has said that when the nightingale sang, silence was pleased. So in the song of the nightingale, we have broadcast something of the silence which all of us in this busy world unconsciously crave and urgently need.'

Such was the huge wave of appreciation that the BBC repeated the experiment later that season. Beatrice commented subsequently that, on meeting King George V: 'before I could even curtsey, [he] said, with such a charming smile: "You have done something I have not been able to do. You have drawn the Empire closer together through the song of the nightingale and your cello."'

Word spreads

And so began Beatrice's double life. In the spring and summer she was 'the Lady of the Nightingales'. There were huge pilgrimages to her home for the weeks of the nightingale's singing. Hundreds of people would turn up every day and night, in complete disregard for the bird's singing hours, and Beatrice and her family improvised an almost 'pop-up' operation, serving tea and cake to the visitors. In the autumn and winter she continued her more traditional cello performances around the UK and Europe.

In 1925 the nightingales returned to the BBC. HMV (famously standing for 'His Master's Voice') joined in and made recordings on ten-inch shellac gramophone disc. They first recorded the nightingales with the Londonderry Air, then came duets with Dvořák's 'Songs My Mother Taught Me' and the nightingales' favourite, 'Chant Hindou'. The recordings, along with general releases of unaccompanied nightingale song and the dawn chorus from Beatrice's garden, were massively popular records, selling in their millions.

The release prompted visitors to come to Foyle Riding from all over the globe once more, including travellers from Canada, Australia, China, Japan and the USA. One letter from a farmer who had left British shores as a boy for New Zealand told Beatrice that it was a prayer answered, to hear that bird sing again. The Harrisons even chartered buses to bring school children and their families from Stepney, east London, who would be fixated on the nightingales. It was a busy time: 'we hired large trestles, cups and saucers, and two huge teapots, one

on each side of the trestle, and every kind of dainty to tempt them ...
One dear mother of ten children told us that the nightingale seemed
to sing for them alone.'

Again Beatrice's performance schedule outside the nightingale sea-
son was packed – she performed dedicated pieces from the likes of
Arnold Bax, Zoltán Kodály and a piece called 'Philomel' by Cyril Scott,
in the UK, Paris, Austria and the Netherlands.

In January 1929 she toured America again, but this time boldly an-
nounced to everyone at her New York concert that they were invited
to come and listen to her nightingales. Apparently she repeated her
address twice and even spelled it out, to avoid any possible confusion.
(On that same trip she brought back two 'small' alligators, which lived
in a tin bath in the living room for a while.) Apparently unable to resist
such an invitation, a huge wave of Americans visited Foyle Riding that
year – more than 2,000 nightingale fans.

Festival fever

In May 1933 Beatrice declared a 'Nightingale Festival' at Foyle Riding in aid of the Royal Society for the Protection of Wild Birds. At that time a Caged Birds Bill was being prepared for Parliament to halt the trade of wild birds at East End markets. To support the endeavour, she opened up the gardens from mid-afternoon until dawn for the price of one shilling, so that everyone could enjoy its abundant birdsong.

The year after this huge endeavour Beatrice's beloved mother passed away. Her father, who had been ill for some time and was never deemed well enough to be told of his wife's demise, followed in 1935. The same year Beatrice's dear friend, the Princess Victoria, died too – and with this seemed to come to an end Beatrice's participation in broadcasts from the house. After so many losses, Foyle Riding became too large and Beatrice downsized and moved elsewhere, so ending her public relationship with the nightingales. By that time she was a household name. Wherever she went, people asked about her nightingales or to see 'old Peter', her infamous cello.

For me, this extraordinary and inspiring woman – who, along with her family, created and nurtured an entire industry around the wonder of one songbird – crystallised that connection to the natural world within so many people. Through Beatrice's passionate advocacy and one small, yet world-changing leap in technology, the 'song of the beak' passed by word of mouth from one person to another. And so it was that more than ninety years ago Britain erupted in conversation about the nightingale. Perhaps it was due to the times: between the wars, when the country had already been through so much and the sense of loss, with which nightingales have always been associated, was close to the surface.

The impact that Beatrice – and her performances with the nightingales – had on the population was huge. As the annual duets became iconic in the popular culture of the time, they became more and more symbolic of Britain's growing love of birds. Today's 1.2 million members of the RSPB are testament to this uniquely British obsession, representing a disproportionately higher subscription than any equivalent organisation in any other country in Europe.

In 1943 Beatrice was asked to join a wartime propaganda comedy film, alongside Laurence Olivier, called *The Demi-Paradise*. Olivier played a Russian inventor, and Penelope Ward his love interest. In Beatrice's scene, the Russians had come to the country to see how well it was faring, and Beatrice was filmed playing with the nightingales, representing an English garden idyll alongside a lake. Clearly, live nightingale song was not a practical option, so a recording of the birds was used.

Beatrice would perform for another decade, often alongside her younger sister Margaret, who was a gifted violin player. They became known for their 'sixpenny' concerts to workers around the country – being devoted, as Beatrice was, to bringing music to the general population. Her final public performance was televised and took place at a Coventry Cathedral fund-raising gala in 1958. She performed several pieces and accompanied Alicia Markova dancing 'The Dying Swan'. She died on 10 March 1965, aged seventy-two.

The bombers

The broadcasts of nightingale song continued, despite Beatrice's non-involvement, right up until May 1942. The BBC was recording the nightingales for their annual performance when the drone of 197 Wellington and Lancaster bombers flying overhead on their way towards

SYLVIA philomela. *Sprosser-Saenger* 1 M.
SYLVIA luscinia. *Nachtigall-Saenger* 2 M.

Mannheim in Germany caused concern. In the interests of national security the broadcast was halted immediately, in case it should act as a warning to the Germans of the planes' approach.

However, although the transmission ceased, the engineers carried on recording that night, and six minutes of nightingale chorus with the steady thrum of the bombers behind it were made into a double-sided record. Side A had the nightingales singing with the planes flying over on their outward journey, and side B the music against the returning bombers – eleven fewer this time. This recording has become one of the most iconic sound-documents over the passage of time. By means of the juxtaposition of the droning engines of war and the lyrical, sweet sound of the birds, a more painful representation of the cruelty of man and the innocent beauty of nature could not be painted.

Urban shift

The twentieth century saw a seismic change in our relationship with birdlife. During the late eighteenth and nineteenth centuries Britain went through an enormous wave of human migration from the country to the city. In the nineteenth century millions left their quiet rural existences to enjoy a newly available modern urban opportunity. New houses swelled the city limits, creating a fully suburban life. This re-imagining of people's domestic home life, once shaped by the patterns of a sometimes unforgiving but always stimulating Mother Nature, was now markedly separate from the natural world.

This period of industrial and social revolution, along with the brutal First World War, represented one of the biggest population shifts in the UK's recent history. Beatrice's nightingale sang into our homes after just a few decades of aspirational urban living, and awoke in many a memory of a more connected life left behind. A radical and transformative piece of new technology – the wireless radio – brought people back to their senses, with a message to the nation to take notice of what had been forgotten. In this urban migration – the biggest leap made since we left our pre-agricultural existence – had we inadvertently become the proverbial bird in a cage? This electric bird spoke to the nation in a language of universality and could be appreciated regardless of class, status or geography. It surpassed religion and politics, as a powerful symbol to which our unreserved affection could be shown. Like an old neighbour returning for tea and a reminisce, he sang his way into the nation's hearts through an open upstairs window.

This musical interruption reminded the nation of how humans and nightingales, and other birds too, had always lived alongside each other. As our circumstances changed, so did our relationship to the outdoors, and especially to birds. This was a notable knock on the door: a request for us to relearn how to let nature back in.

My first duet

In 2014 I noted that we were approaching ninety years since that initial broadcast. On enquiring with the radio people I knew, it seemed that no one at the BBC was aware of this seminal anniversary, despite an online petition to create a nod to the date. So I rapidly wrote an email to Julian May – a longtime BBC documentary maker, producer of *Front Row*, morris dancer and folk lover – to see if I might offer my services to acknowledge this historical moment. Julian, like all good story-hunters, pounced on the idea and said that he would see what he could do. Less than forty-eight hours later (at unheard-of speed for BBC commissions), the BBC had assigned Julian and me fourteen whole minutes to make a documentary. We were commissioned in March, giving us little time to devise, record and edit something suitable enough to be submitted and broadcast in May. We didn't know what we were going to make, so an improvised approach was decided upon: gathering poems and Beatrice interviews, and perhaps taking a folk song or two back to a nightingale, as Beatrice had done, and seeing what happened. But first we needed the nightingales to return to England and start singing again.

The same friends who had taken me to hear nightingales at Arlington Reservoir for the first time all those years ago heard of my endeavour and introduced me to their neighbours. They owned some sensational old coppiced woodland not far from Lewes in East Sussex, which brims with rare butterflies, damselflies and other fast-disappearing local species. Their home is known locally for having nightingales down near a pond that literally gaggles with marsh frogs and marauding water snakes. Happily, they gave us permission to record on their land, and as soon as the nightingales arrived, they called to say that the season had started. The team and I made our way from London to create our homage to Beatrice and her nightingale. Late on a cold, drizzly night three somewhat sceptical string players sheltered with me under umbrellas and we tucked ourselves neatly into the thicket, ready to channel Beatrice and her *bon vivant* spirit.

My romantic expectations of cellos in balmy, aromatic spring woods were firmly tested. But for our nightingale, none of that mattered. He sang regardless of the inclement weather, the musicians' hydrophobia and the intimidating legacy that we were stepping into. As we were almost hugged by the bush, our ears throbbed to the bird's clear song only an arm's reach away. The recording equipment's sound-dial leapt in fits of delight as our nightingale reached full song, bel canto, rising in almost histrionic displays. As a moment's dry respite appeared, we 'trained' musicians took our instruments from their velvet cases, adjusted our sleeves and released our timid sounds to join the proud songster.

As the old folk song 'The Tan Yard Side' grew in confidence and breath, a spell emerged. In the damp shadows of the blackthorn I felt the smiles of the old, old folk singers I'd worshipped, who had carried our ancient songs, grinning all around us. The millennia of nightingales gone before were channelling through this one bird in his insistent liturgy. And that was where it all began for me.

That night was my Damascene moment. I wasn't just listening to the bird; for the first time I entered into a conversation with him. Both our songs came to life, as the power of those ancestral melodies surged through me. It felt new and different, hearing the combination of those two melodies woven into one – more wild and ancient than the sum of their parts.

The documentary *Singing with the Nightingales* was broadcast at 9 p.m. on 19 May 2014 and repeated numerous times afterwards. While we made that boutique homage, I experienced the same thrilling delight that Beatrice must have felt back in 1924, knowing that something we both loved dearly was about to be shared with the nation. I felt a growing suspicion inside me, there and then, that I was going to be stuck in that thicket for a very long time indeed.

CHAPTER FIVE

SONG LINES: OUT OF THE FIRE, INTO THE SHADOWS

The birdsong choruses of dawn and dusk have always been a part of the human aural experience, only to be eventually denied by double glazing and indifference. For those whose whole bodies applaud the full orchestra of birdsong with the musical migrants' return in spring, a larger worldview of this phenomenon is brought to mind by the cosmic conceptualisation of birdsong by the cultural ecologist David Abram.

Imagine boarding a mighty rocket and flying up, above the Earth. Looking down, you would be able to observe the entire circumference of the Earth slowly turning on her orbit: the continents, islands, oceans and weather systems part illuminated. Most notable would be the long shadowline of night, as the daytime Earth shies away from the sun to embrace the darkness, and the dawn emerges on the other side in another land. If you were to focus your ears down on that shadowline, you would hear a wave of birdsong rising longitudinally across the landmass.

There would be a proliferation of the first dawn singers – maybe the blackbird with his first alarm calls, then the wren motoring up – as one by one all the birds lend their voices, until there is an avalanche of sound. Then, as the sun breaks over the horizon, this orchestra settles down to the daytime's baseline chatter. Visualise this sound-wave moving in accordance with that shadowline, like an estuary's tidal bore racing westwards. This wave is more prolific in each hemisphere (North and South) during their respective spring months. Once again that wave of song is repeated, a little more quietly, when the evening turns to gloaming and then to night.

Each chorus has a slightly different relationship to the shadowline. For the dawn chorus, the birds usually start singing when still in darkness, and tail off after full light. At the evening chorus, the sound rises more gradually before full nautical darkness, and finishes while daylight is still visible on the horizon.

The songbirds' instinctive response, acting in total accordance with the position of the planet and the astronomical, nautical and civil twilights, marks the sun's relationship above and beyond the horizon. Throughout early March and into April in the UK, the early migratory species appear one by one, with the highest point of song existing in late April/early May, before waning gradually as summer progresses and the mating season finishes.

Why do birds sing?

The sounds that birds make can be divided into calls and songs. There are numerous motivations for bird calls: there are territorial calls, alarm calls, food calls and mating calls, plus social chatter. Calls are functional; their sound is plain and minimal, and they are common to male and female birds. 'Singing' has more specific motivations – usually mating-related. Its main purpose is territorial 'shouting'. So much of the spring chorus is about the birds affirming their territory, which they assert more stridently at dawn. Birds migrate and travel at night, so most disputes over territories happen in the morning. The early bird has to fight new arrivals for his spot and formidably affirm his position to these intruders. In the evening it's more a case of letting the other birds know 'I'm here, I'm here.' And then there's the mating song – of which the nightingale is the undisputed star. In the daytime the nightingale's refrain is softer and less elaborate.

Much of this information only became known in recent times. The curator Gilbert White (1720–93) is often called England's first 'naturalist' or 'ecologist', and the first birdwatcher, in the modern sense of

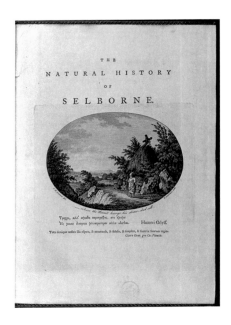

the word. His approach to studying live animals and birds within their natural habitat was unusual at the time, in comparison to the many experts and collectors of taxonomy who took samples from the natural world into the lab. White began his interest in the natural world with a love of gardening and developing new vegetables. For more than forty years he kept a 'Garden Kalendar', which was database-like in his noting of weather patterns, changes of season and associated happenings in the natural world around him. From there grew his wider interest in nature, and in birds in particular. Watching and listening to them, White was able to provide new interpretations and understandings of their rhythms and verify the growing awareness that it was the male songbird that held the ability to sing.

Gilbert White's book, *The Natural History of Selborne*, was first published in 1789 and has remained in print ever since, with 300 editions published to date. This series of letters between White and his esteemed friends described their deep interest in the natural world, encompassing much detail about the workings and relationships of the flora and fauna. With its emotional tones, it inspired the beginnings of a new relationship with nature. White wrote:

> For many months I carried a list in my pocket of the birds that were to be remarked, and, as I rode or walked about my business, I noted each day the continuance or omission of each bird's song; so that I am as sure of the certainty of my facts as a man can be of any transaction whatsoever ... The titlark and yellowhammer breed late, the latter very late; and therefore it is no wonder that they protract their song; for I lay it down as a maxim in ornithology, that as long as there is any incubation going on there is music.

Bird talk

White's inspired observations changed our relationship with birds and nature, bringing together scientific discovery and emotional response. His work anchored our understanding of what lies behind birdsong and other avian compulsions. We can best observe a social side to the nightingales' 'conversation' at night when we hear the males collaborate in their music, and their attempts to show off their breadth of musicality and stamina to each other, as well as to females in the area. As the birds strive to outperform each other, we see why their song has evolved to be so unusual and dynamic.

However, what we appreciate as impressive in a bird isn't necessarily what the birds themselves appreciate in each other. When I take people out to hear the nightingale, those who have never heard him before and expect sweet trills and delicate notes are sometimes surprised – disappointed even – by what they hear. The nightingale's song is an abstract and unusual sound that defies standard birdsong and the birds' use of sound and space. Given the legendary stature placed upon the bird and his music, the expectations of our human ears don't always correspond with the reality.

We may never fully understand the language of the nightingales and their song. Their mystery is part of their allure. I can hear this in their awareness of certain musicians who come with me to play with the birds. With those who have a brightness in their eyes and a deep connection they can channel in their music, the nightingale hears them instantly and responds.

Nightingales have sung with humans for millennia, and I am convinced that this ability for musical kinship has evolved side-by-side, for the epigenetic imprint of their song upon our ancestors is undeniable. Studies proving the correlative benefits of birdsong and mental well-being today feel almost self-evident, when placed in the context of the studied and passionate observations and appreciations of Gilbert White, let alone early humans. But consider this etching of song in the tribal sense on the minds of each generation of early humans growing up bilingual in both our own tongue and the bird languages. Our ancestors were well versed in the inherited wisdom of birdsong and its meaning, not just on a practical level of identification, but through the lens of each individual species' mythology, totemic stature and associated knowledge and prophecy. Like plants and their medicinal properties – the willow's pain-relieving aspirin, the foxglove's heart-stimulating digitalis or the deadly nightshade's pupil-dilating atropine – the song of the nightingale is a sonic equivalent of a deep-tissue massage, a balm for those needing to reroot themselves back in an older way.

Songs forged in flames

The reams of songs, mythologies, sonnets, prose, poems, videos and anecdotes that we have today concerning the nightingale are a mere fragment of the canon of praise and speculation laid upon this bird – much of it, sadly, no longer in evidence or memory. We can now only wonder at how the hearts of our ancestors stirred to the first sounds of nightingale song, and where that song fitted into their cosmologies and worldviews.

To begin to understand how the nightingale and our ancestors shared their lives and wanderings across this Earth, we have to fly backwards on their wings and deeper into our evolutionary past. The signposts are few, but the nightingales' prominence today across the Northern Hemisphere indicates that their wilful song would have accompanied our journeys from prehistory until today. In the UK, as we have seen, the birds have found hospitality in the coppiced woodland, which provided the fuel for our fire. It is fire that we have built our world upon, and it is fire where the next story begins.

Let us go back to when humans began to bring fire into their lives. Fire created a space, a circle of gathering and communication, a ring of protection. It also had the practical effect of broadening our diet and enabling us to eat foods that were nutritionally unavailable unless they were cooked. In turn, humans became better nourished, which had an immense bearing on the development of the brain and its functional ability to progress socially, to create roles and responsibilities in our fledgling societies. What came out of that requisition of fire was the opportunity and necessity to form and develop a more sophisticated means of communication, and thus the natural instinct to employ language as a response to the environment around us.

Social structures emerging within proto-groups meant that we were able to process, describe and interpret our world, and our own role within it. Language and song formed at the same time. The cultivation of the instrument of voice and our oratory skills would have happened in accordance with the sounds of nature around us, and we developed our hunter-gatherer societies in full participation of that sound-world. It taught us, informed us, protected and guided us. Indigenous and tribal communities to this day exemplify an amazing ability to both interpret and imitate the language of animals and birds. There are still examples of robust symbiotic relationships with the animal kingdom – particularly with birds – existing in some communities today. The honey-gatherers of northern Kenya work in partnership with the honeyguides (or bee birds). The birds lead the Boran people to bee colonies in exchange for the larvae-rich beeswax and leftovers after harvesting, as a form of gift exchange. They also understand the human voice's call to work together – thought to be a textbook example of co-evolution between species.

Humans have, subconsciously and consciously, utilised that under-standing to read deeper into the landscape and meteorology than was ever possible with our human perceptions. Bird language and behaviour were our indicators of oncoming change, weather, jeopardy, the prox-imity of predators and similar vulnerabilities, or prophecies of fortune. For example, during general daytime activity, should we hear the ambi-ent birdsong fall silent or conversely rise into alarm calls, then the ripple of alarms can be interpreted backwards to the source of the disturbance. Through the tiniest levels of variation, a sharp-eared human tracker can tell exactly what predator is coming, from where, and in what state of hunt or rest – prowling or flying – that creature is. Through the bird's song our ears are able to reach deep into the landscape.

Few cultures throughout history have not had a relationship with birds. Their significance is embedded somewhere in most of the great mythologies and creation myths of old. Birds act as prophetic messengers from the spiritual realm and represent transformation, enlightenment and foresight; our connection with birds' 'superior' or hidden knowledge is part of our wider cultural bond.

Humans re-creating bird music

Birds were the conduit through which our earliest known music was made. The first distinct evidence of human musicality was discovered in caves in southern Germany in 2004. These ancient bone flutes were made of mammoth ivory, and other similar instruments were created from the bones of a mute swan and a griffon vulture. These wonderful examples of humans making music for, and with, each other by means of the bird suggests an inextricable connection between the music that *Homo sapiens* would have heard and their desire to re-create that sound for themselves. Tests dates the flutes to approximately 42,000 years old – roughly the period when modern humans reached Europe from Africa. Professor Nicholas Conard of Tübingen University said, 'These finds demonstrate the presence of a well-established musical tradition at the time when modern humans colonized Europe.'[1] These primitive flutes have musical scales bored into them that are by no means rudimentary, random or atonal. Instead there are deliberate intervals between the notes, illustrating an already sophisticated musical articulacy, evidence of an evolved and intentional expression.

[1] N. J. Conard, M. Malina, S. C. Munzel, 'New flutes document the earliest musical tradition in southwestern Germany', *Nature*, 6 August 2009, 460 (7256): 737–40.

Simultaneous evolution

Today nightingales connect us back to our ancestral motherland, their flesh and feathers grown from the same soil as us. I am sure nightingales would have been heard almost continuously in the slow 'northern route dispersal' (the most prominent migration theory of anatomically modern human beings) up from the Horn of Africa along the Great Rift Valley into Ethiopia, Turkey, Israel, Egypt and Jordan. It seems unlikely there would have been a time when humankind wasn't listening to their seasonal song. Could nightingales have forged their migration patterns alongside human routes northwards, or did humans follow the migration routes of our migrant bird neighbours?

At the hands of early humankind, nightingales would have benefited greatly from our wielding of fire upon the landscape. This releasing of wildfire, and the subsequent regrowth, created the grasslands, scrub and pasture necessary for the large herds of the prey that we liked to hunt. The dense woodlands that prevailed across the northern European landmass could not support grass-dependent ruminants and other herbivores, but human-assisted adaption of the environment meant that a songbird-friendly landscape would have burgeoned incidentally.

How have nightingales' migration patterns collaborated with our own migration? We might never know where in prehistory the nightingale sang within the African landmass. Did populations remain all year round, or had they been migrating for hundreds of thousands of years before the evolution of the apes? And did the nightingale always sing its particular song as we hear it today?

There may have been other night-birds at that time. Perhaps the nightingale succeeded other more beautiful songbirds of the night, which were less adaptable to the changing landscape. But I wonder also whether the thrust northwards of humankind, and the way we forged the landscape as we progressed, brought the nightingale with us. Our practice of scorching the ground, opening up the landscape, created prolific regrowth in the charred soils and, like coppicers today, brought prime habitat into consideration for nightingales to proliferate within. Maybe the volumed reach of the nightingale's voice adapted due to a fast-expanding territory, where females needed to hear their suitors while flying over miles of dense forest, listening for lone males dispersed across newly colonised habitats.

I must caveat this narrative by making clear that this is my own imaginative stroll into the many unknowable possibilities of how species interplay with one another. It is pure conjecture how the nightingale evolved in dynamic, fluid ecosystems over time – being, like all species, one that moves and adapts in response to trophic cascades and wildly shifting climates. Whatever the interaction, it's safe to say there has always been interplay at most points during the approximately 300,000 years that *Homo sapiens* has been finding his way 'out of Africa'.

George Monbiot theorises that the robin's fearlessness of and affection for humans, especially the gardener, is due to the fact that it has become dependent on us. He postulates that the robin had exactly this same relationship with the Northern Hemisphere megafauna – the mammoths and woolly rhinos that passed through the woodland, uprooting trees and tearing up the ground to expose worms and similar fuel. The robin's reliance on these excavators became established. Now it is the human spade and hand, opening up the ground, that the robin has replaced in its affections.

In any case the 'special relationship' between bird and human is fluid and dynamic. The nightingales' population spread would have grown and shrunk like that of any species, in accordance with glacial and interglacial periods, and with the footfall of human and beast that wove their lives around this bird. Nightingales can't survive in thick, dense woodland with a heavy, overshadowing canopy. Consider then what the landscape of Europe would have looked like, pre-humankind. Perhaps it featured such dense forest that nightingales didn't appear there, until humans arrived and developed a mosaic of woodland pasture. Or *did* the nightingale survive in these wooded environments, but simply evolved away from this habitat as new scrubby opportunities appeared and the landscape adapted, bit by bit, to new influences and the new fire-fingered, five-fingered visitor?

All the above theories can, of course, similarly be applied to the blackcap or willow warbler, and not just the nightingale. All bird populations benefited or suffered – some even perished – in the wake of human progress. New Zealand's moa birds became extinct between the thirteenth and sixteenth centuries, after eons of contact with the Maori settlers; as did the dodo on the island of Mauritius when Western sailors brought rats, dogs and monkeys, all of which were alien to that environment. The rock dove, conversely – once a wild European bird – has flourished as city buildings have boomed, providing a new and ideal habitat.

Shadows of the nightingale in the ancient world

As I hear the spirited sound of a nightingale's song, which seems to declare the nocturnal land alive on a warm spring night, I feel a tug at the same archaic nerve that shivers with awe when I see the bison, oxen and wild-horse herds painted on the Chauvet or Lascaux cave walls. When I look at those pigment-painted fauna on the cave walls I feel a distinct, intense sense of 'animal power', just as I do when I sing with the nightingale, deep in that blackthorn bush. I imagine the suet candles illuminating those subterranean Chauvet galleries more than 30,000 years ago (and perpetually interacted with, shamanically, for many thousands of years afterwards) and how the paintings governed a deep allegiance, and affirmed a series of pre-denominational identities in each beast. Shining in the dark then were those big cats and cave-cows; and today, for those of us with such animistic tendencies, there are our bush-birds: both *'son et lumière'* to alternate gods, each a narrator to a million forgotten stories that we told about them.

Nightingales, like all birds, have always been with us. Like the circles we formed ourselves into around those ancestral fires, and the circles created by birds of prey riding hot thermals skywards, this spiralling geometry echoes deep within our creation stories. 'The Everlasting Circle', one of Britain's and Europe's oldest-known songs, tells of this cycle of life in a mythic 'chasing of one's own tail'. This song's conceit is echoed in the ancient Egyptians' ouroboros symbol 1,400 years NO– the image of the snake eating its own tail. It is found more locally in the never-ending world-within-a-world of the bird within the egg, within the tree, as collected in folk-song form by the Victorian song collector Cecil Sharp in Priddy, Somerset, in 1905. Here the words of local man John Vincent were sung in an accumulating form, so that the song grows longer with each verse:

> In the Merryshire wood there growed a tree,
> And a very fine tree was he
> And the tree growed in the Merryshire wood
> In the Merryshire wood, in the Merryshire wood
> And the tree growed in the Merryshire wood.

And on that tree there was a limb
And on that limb there was a branch
And on that branch there was a spray
And on that spray there was a nest
And in that nest there was an egg
And in that egg there was a bird
And on that bird there was a feather
And on that feather there was a bed
And on that bed there was a maid
And on that maid there was a man
And the tree growed in the Merryshire wood
In the Merryshire wood, in the Merryshire wood
And the tree growed in the Merryshire wood.

The nightingale, although in no way explicitly suggested, is surely woven into that archetypal circle bird: 'within our fire is the wood, within those woods is the bird, within the bird is the song, and within that song is the fire', I might suppose. As with many of our oldest well-sprung songs, there exists an infusion of such a sentiment within the words found in the mouths of singers like John Vincent, just a century ago. Despite the attempts of Church and State to suppress such primal ideas throughout Britain's repressive history, they have persisted in the vernacular in exactly the same way that the nightingale's song has persisted in unwanted scrapland and managed 'reserves' that are not fully colonised by economic opportunity. Folk song and birdsong alike, surviving in the margins and at the edges of 'man's' dominance.

Philomela luscinia. Linn.

Cromska, U Bresslau. Wien.

CHAPTER SIX

SPRING COMES: CELEBRATIONS, CEREMONY AND SEDUCTION

... The nest is made a hermit's mossy cell.

    Snug lie her curious eggs in number five,

    Of deadened green, or rather olive brown;

    And the old prickly thorn-bush guards them well.

    So here we'll leave them, still unknown to wrong,

    As the old woodland's legacy of song.

from 'The Nightingale's Nest' by John Clare

Our nightingale is one of the early migrant heralds of spring. He arrives in the UK around 12 April, with usually only a day or two of variation in the timing as he waits for a southerly wind from France. At that time of year the country is a still-wintered landscape and the trees are quite bare when he begins his song.

There's a sort of knowingness in the air when the nightingale appears, an expectancy – the land declaring that the game is on. While we beat our carpets on the first sunny days and venture out without overcoats to bare our skin to the growing sun, the nightingale calls his song out throughout his domain, enticing in the new season.

I like to think that as the tree saps are drawn, so the ever-growing chorus of birds is an extension of that flow of energy, in turn drawing up the bluebells from their earthy cocoons below. The birdsong calls from their slumber the early flowerers – the lesser celandine and the wood anemone – confirming, at last, that spring is not a false hope.

Nightingales favour blackthorn bushes as their preferred nesting ground, and in the cold early spring nights this dense, thorny scrub appears like coral reefs, phosphorescent in the moonlight. These pillows of blossom softly defy the plant's thorny impenetrability as they issue a mild, powdery scent. If you breathe deeply when you are out at night, your nose might notice a bouquet of pulverised pollen in the air. Should a clear sky and moon-phase conspire, then the endless stretches of blossom combine with the nightingale's song bursting out from within, to become simply one of the most extraordinary occurrences in the English landscape. A black-and-white world turned luminous and radiant, revealing bursts of song – energetic surges like filaments of electricity powering the fields while everything else is in sleep mode. Nightingales bring their home alive, agitating and activating it, little sparklers of sound, best heard when impossible to be seen.

The messenger

Not many lifetimes ago, our forefathers and mothers lived in a relationship with the land that was indisputedly more reciprocal and dependent than it is today. They had a radically more direct and self-sufficient connection, unsupported by today's technological and chemical abilities to 'manage' the harvest. Barely a hundred years ago a failed harvest could prove fatal to a family or even to a whole community (in fact this is still the case for many outside the ultra-developed Western world). One's prospects of survival, after taxes and tithes had been paid, were dangerously precarious.

Maintaining a home and feeding one's children and elders formed a complicated and uncertain lottery. After a long winter the grain stores were bare, the stored fruits and roots of the previous year's labours would be gone, and malnourishment was an unwelcome guest in many a rural home. Those first heaven-sent shoots of spring were extraordinarily potent and filled with nutrients. Often the elder tree's first leaf, the early nettle shoots or the starch-rich roots of the lesser celandine were sought out, to add much-needed richness to a stale, winter-weary set of preserved staples.

THE NIGHTINGALE.

And so as the spray of hawthorn leaves appears in tight fists, so too does the nightingale. His arrival comes as a sweet accompaniment to thankful homesteads who made it through another winter. It seems clear why nearly 3,000 years ago the Greek poet Sappho named her 'spring's messengers' as 'the sweet-voiced nightingale'.

Every year I, too, experience that same cocktail of emotions felt for thousands of years before me. It is as if the nightingale song is embedded in human genetics like a soundtrack to a cascade of joy and triumph, of gratitude for survival and coming plentitude, of rejuvenation and rebirth. The nightingale's music is inextricably linked with the annual cycle of restoration, death and regrowth. These themes are implicitly, and sometimes explicitly, expressed in the variegated calendar events and ceremonies, such as May Day, Beltane, Pace Egging, Easter and the many other springtime folk customs in the UK, across Europe and beyond.

Feasts and celebrations

So soon after the bird's arrival comes May Day, a tradition much diminished now in its significance and practice, but once a focal day of celebration for the arrival of 'summer' across the Northern Hemisphere. The day was a festival for all, reflected in its contemporary co-incidence with International Workers' Day. In the UK rituals such as choosing the May Queen (a modern ancestral representation of Flora, the Roman god of flowers) are still practised by communities across the country. Similar celebration rites are carried out across Europe on 1 May and the surrounding days, to mark the triumph of summer over winter and to ask for protection of animals and crops. The maypole is an ancient tradition associated with much debauchery in the gatherings around these enormous totemic and fecund symbols on May nights. The rituals of carolling and 'well-dressing' – thanking the gods by decorating water sources with floral garlands and blessing the water – are idiosyncrasies that remain in practice in our communities to this day.

In Cornwall's Padstow, the atavistic 'Obby 'Ossing on May Day – where the 'Obby 'Oss (a black, white and red hobby horse) is paraded through the streets, before lying down to 'die' and then being revived, all accompanied by day- and night-singing – continues with the 'Padstow May Song':

> ... Up flies the kite, down falls the lark-o
> Aunt Ursula Birdwood she has an old ewe
> And she died in her own park-o

Unite and unite and let us all unite

For summer is a-comin' today.

And whither we are going we all will unite

In the merry morning of May.

Similarly, cuckoo celebrations and fairs were traditionally held late in April to mark that bird's arrival. Marsden in West Yorkshire still has a Cuckoo Day (complete with maypole); and *The Times* features a letter pronouncing the first cuckoo heard each year. Heathfield in East Sussex annually holds the Heffle Cuckoo Fair (running since 1315) to celebrate the coming in of spring, by releasing a live 'cuckoo' each year (nowadays replaced by a pigeon).

The nights were filled with merry-making, and nightingales – much more common then, of course – would have sung along with these and many other ceremonies, in the thickets and woods around the

"JACK-IN-THE-GREEN" – A MAY-DAY SCENE SIXTY YEARS AGO

villages. Those lengthening, warming nights would have been spent in gatherings, country dances and frivolity. The fecund days of early May were once magnificently licentious and orgiastic occasions, which went hand-in-hand with the rituals and celebrations of much more sexually unrestrained pre-religious communities. These wild practices, eventually smothered by religious Puritanism, all played out through the warming spring nights across Europe and southern England, to the accompaniament of the nightingale's mating song in the surrounding greenery.

The nightingale is not part of the dusk chorus, so he isn't present at early-evening gatherings. He adorns the ribald after-dark disorder instead. The male, or cock, nightingale does sing during the day, but it is at night that the luring of the female bird truly takes hold. Many years ago expeditions to hear the nightingale occurred, as they still do to this day. For young lovers, this was a part of the romance.

The Quarry Bank nightingale

George Dunn (1887–1975), a chain-maker from the Black Country who was also a renowned folk-song carrier and source of oral history, recalled the local Quarry Bank nightingale:

> The nightingale sings at night. Wheer we are now I should say for fifty acres it was all woodland. We used to call this the bottom wood and that up theer the top wood. One summer, just for a bit o' devilment, father went an' took a nightingale up to the top wood and

for a fortnight there came crowds to 'ear it. 'E took a nightingale up 'isself. 'E did it! Father went up to the wood one night and 'e whistled a nightingale. Our woods they grow like a jungle and it was easy for 'im to conceal 'imself. It went on for about a fortnight until it got too big to 'andle. There come too many people down at night. From Dudley and Brierley Hill and Wolver'ampton. It was summut special. When it got too 'ot 'e dae go no more. The nightingale dae sing no more. That hoax was never known, only t'us kids. 'E towd us about it.

I like to imagine how the nightingale was adopted by young lovers as a beacon in the landscape where they could meet. Like the Quarry Bank nightingale, the old stories tell of young lovers who would slip out back doors to meet in the darkness beyond the gaze of their families. The nightingale's song can be heard up to a mile away, so they would arrange to meet where the nightingale was singing in a particular grove. Perhaps there was the further advantage of being able to hide the squeals of delight beneath his strident song …

So the nightingale entered our folk songs as a symbol of illicit behaviour – often the voice of seduction, melancholy and bittersweet love. Several of our great folk songs tell of lovers walking together and sitting down to listen to the nightingales, as if this was their only intention – as in 'Green Bushes', a traditional song sung by Walter Pardon of Norfolk:

> As I was a-walking one morning in Spring
> To hear the birds whistle and the nightingales sing
> I met a young damsel and sweetly sang she
> 'Down by the green bushes, he thinks to meet me.'

> I stepped up to her and this I did say
> 'Why wait you so long, love, on this sunny day?'
> 'My true-love, my true-love,' so sweetly sang she,
> 'Down by the green bushes, he thinks to meet me.'

On the nights when I indulge my romantic whim to seek this poetry echoing through the woods, I am aware that I am driven by more than simply the need to experience something beautiful, fleeting or ephemeral. Every night I find new purpose and enquiry in the primal power of the darkness and this bird. These quests make me ask: what is it that calls us into the woods, into nature? What do people come looking for? For me, the nightingale has been a powerful lure to give up my own urban roots and go almost feral for six weeks each year. But why? Is it just the song, the myths, the romance of the night-time? Perhaps I do it for the same reason the birds come to us: out of instinct and opportunity.

To assume the nightingale's motivation to be only procreation and feeding would be a half-witted and utterly anthropomorphic reduction of a highly complex, specialised creature. Like this bird, so specific in his tastes, I have found my niche as an artist in an ecosystem of noise-makers and performers, to gather my species, to feast and express our notions of love through song and prose. I take great pleasure in acting as an agent for that experience between nightingales and humans, such is my gregarious nature. Deeper still, I have found for myself a dependence on this bird in the same way that all species have a dependence on one another – a creative symbiosis. Each year I spin myself further back into the web of nature, into this ancient seasonal occurrence. Creating this ritual with the birds binds them deeper into a connection with our world, and our world into theirs.

Every visit to hear a nightingale starts with a long walk in the dark. The night-song, when we do hear it, opens up and flushes the senses, demanding a glorious quiet in oneself. The grand finale of one species' annual migration home instigates the journey of another, and so the ceremony goes on, over and over again. Each night, as a group or sometimes alone, through attentive listening and subtle, songful improvisation, we imprint our presence and an expression of our truth onto this bird and, as John Keats would say, his 'melodious plot'; and in turn we have that 'beechen green' imprinted upon us.

Very often what I encounter is a sense of dissolving – especially of the separation between the worlds of humans and nature. It's a lesson in mindfulness, but also in getting out of one's mind and into another's. When migrations happen in nature, the character or the actual physiology of that species can change in response to the environment or phase of their life: for example, when salmon move from salt water to sweet water; or the pupation of monarch-butterfly larvae. In the nightingale's company we can leave one state of mind, become unravelled and then reconstituted – realigned, affirmed and renewed. At nearly one o'clock in the morning, as a group of us leave the thicket of a night's singing with the nightingales and return to that place I call the 'unreal world', I will find that my entire group has grown a small pair of wings; some are even flying.

Pl. 646.

1. Rossignol 2. Son Nid. 3. Rubiette (Rouge gorge).

CHAPTER SEVEN

BALLADS, BROADSIDES AND BERKELEY SQUARE: FOLKSONGS AND NIGHTINGALES IN BRITAIN

When it comes to folk song, the nightingale tends to reveal more about the culture that is singing about him or her than about the actual nature of the bird. In the UK nightingales are given a variety of guises that reveal the diversity of ways in which the British project the national character onto nature. These depictions range from a bite-sized, comical creature to the witness of heart's sorrow – as is more common in the Mediterranean tradition. Internationally, it's surprising how base some of the fancying of this bird becomes as we travel west into the UK, compared to the nightingales' association with devotional music and melodrama further east in Europe and Asia.

The Roud Index, compiled by Steve Roud, is a taxonomical system of folk song covering the entire repertoire of songs, and every instance of a song being noted, recorded, collected, printed and published across the English-speaking world. The index hosts 570 songs with 'Nightingale' in the title. Admittedly, many of these are the names of ships, waltzes and other dances, or tunes known simply as 'The Nightingale', but this is a prolific number compared to the 377 larks, 124 hawks, 117 pigeons, 116 sparrows, 112 thrushes, 73 turtle doves and 137 chickens. In fact the nightingale is only beaten by blackbirds, with 611 instances on record, mostly due to the massive popularity of the song 'If I Was a Blackbird', known by almost every folk singer from whom songs were ever collected.

Every country seems to have sense of ownership of the bird; that much is universal. Wales has not known a nesting nightingale (*eos* in the Welsh language) for a very long time – if ever – yet the bird is still accepted in song as if it is a common visitor, a staple of the spring morning. In the Welsh song 'Little Mountain Birds' the emotional lyricism feels much more connected to the tone of the European-nightingale folk songs than to its British counterparts, as we see below.

Adar Mân y Mynydd / Little Mountain Birds

Yr eos a'r glân hedydd　　　　The nightingale and the spotless lark
Ac adar mân y mynydd,　　　　And the little birds of the mountain,
A ewch chi'n gennad at Liw'r Haf　Wilt thou go as messenger to summer's
　　　　　　　　　　　　　　　　　　　　　　colour
Sy'n glaf o glefyd newydd?　　　Which is suffering from a new illness?

Does gennyf ddim anrhegion　　　I have no gifts
Na jewels drud i'w danfon　　　　Nor expensive jewels to send
I ddwyn i'ch cof yr hwn a'ch câr　To remind you of him who loves you,
Ond pâr o fenig gwynion.　　　　But a pair of white gloves.

Yr adar mân fe aethant,　　　　The little birds did go
I'w siwrnai bell hedasant,　　　On their distant journey they flew
Ac yno ar gyfer gwely Gwen　　　And then facing Gwen's bed
Hwy ar y pren ganasant.　　　　On the tree they sang.

Dywedai Gwen, lliw'r ewyn,　　　Said Gwen the colour of the foam
'Och fi pa beth yw'r 'deryn　　　'Ah me, what thing is the bird
Sydd yma'n tiwnio'n awr mor braf　Which is here warbling now so prettily
A minnau'n glaf ar derfyn?'　　　And I terminally ill?'

'Cenhadon ym, gwnewch goelio　　'We are messengers please believe
Oddi wrth y mwyn a'ch caro,　　　Sent on behalf of the one who loves you
Gael iddo wybod ffordd yr y'ch,　To let him know how you are faring
Ai mendio'n wych ai peidio.'　　Whether you are growing pale or not.'

'O dwedwch wrtho'n dawel	'Tell him softly
Mai byr fydd hyd fy hoedel,	That short will be my lifetime,
Cyn diwedd hyn o haf, yn brudd	Before this summer ends sadly
Â'n gymysg bridd a grafel.	I am going to be among soil and gravel.'[2]

In England, too, the nightingale is rarely far from lovers and physical acts of love – be it in 'the valleys below' or 'down by some green bushes'. There are several significant songs in the UK that feature principally the nightingale, but no song better summarises that association of the bird with licentious, promiscuous behaviour and questionable morality than the one known simply as 'The Nightingale'. This was one of the most popular English folk songs among traditional singers and was widely reappraised during the British folk revival from the 1950s onwards, often with the alternative name of 'The Bold Grenadier', 'The Soldier and the Lady' or 'One Morning in May'.

The Nightingale

One morning, one morning, one morning in May,
I spied a young couple, they were making their way.
One was a maiden so bright and so fair
and the other was a soldier and a brave volunteer.

'Good morning, good morning, good morning,' said he,
'And where are you going my pretty lady?'
'I'm going out a-walking on the banks of the sea
Just to see the water's glide and hear the nightingale sing.'

---

[2] Translated by Richard B. Gillion, and collected by one John Morris in the Ffestiniog area.

Now they had not been standing but a minute or two
When out of his knapsack a fiddle he drew
And the tune that he played made the valleys all ring,
'Oh hark,' cried the maiden. 'Hear the nightingale sing.'

'Oh maiden, fair maiden, 'tis time to give o'er.'
'Oh no, kind soldier, please play one tune more
For I'd rather hear your fiddle at the touch of one string
Than to see the waters glide and hear the nightingale sing.

'Oh soldier, kind soldier, will you marry me?'
'Oh no, pretty maiden, that never shall be.
I've a wife down in London and children twice three,
Two wives and the army's too many for me.

'Well, I'll go back to London and I'll stay there for a year,
It's often that I'll think of you, my little dear.
And if ever I return it will be in the spring
Just to see the waters glide and hear the nightingale sing.
To see the waters glide and hear the nightingale sing.'

Then with kisses and compliments he took her round the middle,
And out of his knapsack he drawed forth a fiddle,
And he played her such a fine tune as made the groves and valleys ring,
'Hark, hark,' says the fair maid. 'How the nightingales sing.'[3]

This classic song of love and deceit boasts 133 different versions on record in the UK, and even more in renderings in the US (such as the cowboy's

---

[3] Collected by H. E. D. Hammond from William Bartlett in Wimborne Union (workhouse), Dorset, 1905.

lustful attempts in 'The Wild Rippling Water', as it is sometimes known there). The British phrases 'he drew out his fiddle' and with the 'touch of one string and the nightingale sings' became particularly popular in North American folk song. Interestingly, these versions sometimes include an extra warning verse for women to take care among the menfolk:

> Come all you young maidens, take warning from me;
> Never place your affections in a cowboy too free;
> He'll go away an' leave you like mine did me;
> Leave you to rock cradles, sing 'Bye-o-babee';
> Leave you to rock cradles, sing 'Bye-o-babee'.

I interpret such warnings as additional small print for the singer's intended audience – these songs come from a pre-contraceptive era, in a far more puritanical society than the old world where the song originated. Even if you didn't know what the nightingale's song sounded like (as country Americans wouldn't have done in those days), you would at least know that men who lead you off to hear the nightingale, or want to play you their fiddle, are probably to be avoided.

Since the twentieth-century revival onwards, 'The Nightingale' has been recorded by a huge range of popular stars, from James Taylor to the Dubliners, plus a magnificent fully orchestrated version by Jo Stafford. It even made the big screen in the 1967 adaptation of *Far from the Madding Crowd*, in which it was sung by Isla Cameron, with a brooding Julie Christie and Alan Bates behind.

There is another classic song of a woman swapping the lover she expected to meet down by the 'Green Bushes' (as the song is known) for a more profligate stranger, who appears in this scene quite by accident. This tale, rich in flippant imprudence, appears scandalous and immoral in its depiction. However, when you begin to explore the courtship competitiveness of our nightingale, and other birds too, it is actually quite standard behaviour. Is this also a song about humans imitating nature? And were the singers of the past well aware of the duality of technique in human and bird courtship?

Green Bushes

As I was a-walking one morning in Spring
To hear the birds whistle and the nightingales sing
I met a young damsel and sweetly sang she,
'Down by the green bushes, he thinks to meet me.'

'I'll buy you fine dresses and a new silken gown
I'll buy you a fine petticoat with a flounce to the ground
If you will promise you'll be true to me
And leave the green bushes, and marry to me.'

Traditional folk songs in the UK take the form of narrative sung poems called 'ballads', which would largely have been passed down the generations orally, through families and communities, but often originated in broadsides or broadsheets. These were affordable one-page printed song sheets, which were mass-produced, with popular news and tales played out in song form. The favourites that made it into circulation in a local area informed a rich source of folk-song heritage that still exists today in the oral tradition, mostly amongst Gypsy Travellers, with a unique exception in the Copper family, as mentioned below.

Another major nightingale folk song is 'Sweet Nightingale' (also known as 'To a Nightingale' or 'Down in the Valley Below'), which is referred to as the 'Cornish Anthem'. Considering that the bird is not known to have nested in Cornwall within living memory, it is pertinent that the song is so significant there. My late teacher, the song collector Peter Kennedy, apparently traced its arrival to Cornish lead miners, who brought it back to Cornwall after learning it while working in German lead mines. It was apparently then translated from Cornish into English in the nineteenth century, keeping the same tune, which sounds about as English as can be.

A version collected by Cecil Sharp from a Captain Jack Short in the early 1920s is by far the most elegant, in my opinion. Short, from north Somerset, was one of the last surviving sea-shanty singers to share his songs with a collector. These were variants of the many classic songs that evolved in that musically flourishing period just before sailing ships made way for steamers. The technological advancements in sailing ships provided new working techniques, which created new rhythms and thus new songs in response. Coupled with this, far out at sea local folk songs were thrown into a melting pot of cultures, in the mouths of sailors and shanty singers like Short. Anglo-Irish songs or words would be influenced by the rhythms, melodies and song styles of a crew with heritages as diverse as Native America, the Caribbean, West Africa, South America and even Maori New Zealand. In Captain Short, we find a song carrier who travelled with his version of 'Sweet Nightingale' further even than the nightingales themselves.

Sweet Nightingale *(An Eos Whek)*

My sweetheart, come along,
Don't you hear the fond song,

THE NIGHTINGALE

The sweet notes of the nightingale flow?
Don't you hear the fond tale
Of the sweet nightingale
As she sings in the valley below?
As she sings in the valley below?

Pretty Betty, don't fail,
For I'll carry your pail
Safe home to your cot as we go.
You shall hear the fond tale
Of the sweet nightingale
As she sings in the valley below.
As she sings in the valley below.

Pray let me alone, I have hands of my own;
Along with you, sir, I'll not go.
For to hear the fond tale
Of the sweet nightingale
As she sings in the valley below.
As she sings in the valley below.

Pray sit yourself down
With me on the ground,
On this bank where the primroses grow.
You shall hear the fond tale
Of the sweet nightingale
As she sings in the valley below.
As she sings in the valley below.

This couple agreed

To be married with speed

And soon to the church they did go.

Never more she's afraid

For to walk in the shade

Or to sit in these valleys below.

The Copper family

There are few celebrants of the majesty of nature finer than the Copper family of Rottingdean in East Sussex. To this day they are the living custodians of English song and verse and have records dating back to the 1600s of their family singing. Known as the 'first family of folk music', the Coppers came to prominence in the 1930s through the work of one of the principal family members, Bob Copper (1915–2004). With his brothers, cousins and relatives, Bob sang the great Sussex shepherding songs, plough songs and old ballads. And the family is unique not just for their unbroken oral line of music, but because they sing in harmony, quite unlike any other documented instance of traditional British song.

Solo, unaccompanied verse is the way British indigenous song has always been heard. Instrumental or harmony backing began only relatively recently, at the end of the nineteenth and early twentieth centuries, with revivalists' piano arrangements, orchestration and choral settings in published books, and later through the recording industry with guitars, and so on. The Coppers are therefore unusual in their singing tradition, with their fixed three-part harmonies. Bob Copper was employed by the BBC to collect songs in and around Sussex and became a well-known orator, writer of Sussex pastoral experiences and chronicler of the lives of those living on the land. He wrote a series of books – *A Song for Every Season* being his best known – which painted a rather romantic depiction of the old land workers and shepherds he knew. Many of the Coppers' songs testify to the joy of the countryside and of the chalk downs where they lived.

One of their best-loved songs, 'Birds in the Spring' (known in other versions as 'Down the Green Grove' and 'Early One May Morning'), is an extraordinary hymn to birdsong in itself, but holds the nightingale principally at its heart.

> ... And the song of the nightingale echoed all round.
> Their note was so charming, their notes were so clear ...
> No music, no songster can with them compare.

Birds in the Spring

> One May morning early I chanced for to roam,
> And strolled through the field by the side of the grove,
> It was there I did hear the harmless birds sing.
> And you never heard so sweet,
> And you never heard so sweet,
> You never heard so sweet as the birds in the spring.
>
> At the end of the grove I sat myself down
> And the song of the nightingale echoed all round.
> Their note was so charming, their notes were so clear
> No music, no songster,

no music, no songster,

No music, no songster can with them compare.

All you that come here the small birds to hear,

I'll have you pay attention, so pray all draw near.

And when you're growing old you will have this to say,

That you never heard so sweet,

You never heard so sweet,

You never heard so sweet as the birds on the spray.

'Birds in the Spring' was first noted down from the Copper family back in 1899 in the *Journal of the Folk-Song Society*. Reflecting on this song now, in a time of crashing bird populations, the last lines of retrospective adoration from the old to the younger self seem more pertinent than ever.

'The Nightingale', 'Sweet Nightingale' and 'Birds in the Spring' are three of the most well-known and loved nightingale songs in the British tradition, although the bird also appears in many other beautiful songs. The Coppers also sang of our bird in 'Sweet Lemeney' and 'The Haymakers'.

Sweet Lemeney

As I was a-walking one fine summer's morning

The fields and the meadows they looked so green and gay

And the birds they were singing, so pleasantly adorning,

So early in the morning at the break of the day.

Oh hark, oh hark, how the nightingale is singing,

The lark she is taking her flight all in the air.

> On yonder green bower the turtle doves are building,
> The sun is just a-glimmering, arise my dear!

This was a popular English country song, even being noted down in 1820 by Thomas Hardy in Dorset, and with versions found as far north as Yorkshire – way beyond nightingale territory – with suggestions that it was Irish in origin.

The collections of broadsides that we still find in libraries abound with many thousands of mentions of nightingales as decoration and metaphor. 'Birds of Harmony', or 'The Bird Lamentation', which is written in the voices of the birds themselves, is a magnificent telling from the 1680s of the great conversation of each bird's songful complaint:

> 'Oh,' said the pretty nightingale,
> 'Come listen awhile unto my tale.
> While others do sleep I sit and mourn,
> Leaning my breast against the thorn.'

This ballad imports the Persian icon of the bird and the thorn, suggesting influences of the East on English folk culture. One of the most fascinating English folk songs in which the nightingale has left his mark is 'The Haymakers' (also sung by the Copper family with the title 'The Pleasant Month of May'). The first appearance occurred in a broadside from 1656 entitled 'The countrey peoples felicitie' or 'A brief description of pleasures'. This song has lasted well, with collectors finding many versions among singers of the late-nineteenth and early twentieth centuries. However, the lyrics of one verse that, over time, seem to have corrupted into a new meaning feature the song of the nightingale. The original 1600s text has these lines:

'Sweet jug, jug, jug, jug, jug, jug, jug,'
The nightingale did sing,
Whose noble voice made all rejoice
As they were making hay.

When collected recently, this had transformed into a very different 'jug'. The Romany singer Levi Smith was recorded near Epsom, Surrey, in 1974 singing his version with the lines:

Oh jug, oh sweet jug,
Oh, drink to the morning dew.
But we all chucked down our forks and rakes,
And we left off making hay.

This is a wonderful example of folk-song evolution in action. The onomatopoeic use of 'jug, jug, jug' is a highly inventive and accurate musical use of the rhythm of our bird's song, often found in nightingale poetry (most notably from T. S. Eliot).

I often sing a song called 'Lovely Molly' at nightingale gatherings. It comes from the Robertsons, a Scottish Traveller family, and was sung by both Stanley Robertson and his cousin Lizzie Higgins. Both learned the song from their respective aunt and mother, Jeannie Robertson, MBE, the legendary ballad singer who is cited by many as one of the most important singers of the twentieth century. Jeannie, in turn, learned it from the renowned folklorist Hamish Henderson. Having spent four years apprenticed to Stanley and inheriting his songs, I am pretty sure that he had never heard a nightingale, yet this truly Scottish song still feels utterly knowing of the bird's beauty and importance. The chorus's last two lines could just as easily have been sung by, and about, the birds themselves:

Lovely Molly

I once was a ploughboy, but a soldier I'm now,
I courted lovely Molly, as I followed the plough;
I courted lovely Molly, from the age of sixteen,
But now I must leave her, and serve James the king.

Oh Molly, lovely Molly, I delight in your charms,
And there's many's the long night you have lay in my arms.
But if ever I return again, it will be in the Spring
When the mavis[4] and the turtle dove and the nightingale sing.

---

[4] 'Mavis' is the colloquial name for the song thrush, derived from the Middle English *mavys* and the Old French *mauvis*.

You can go to the market, you can go to the fair;
You can go to church on Sunday, and meet your new love there.
But if anybody loved you half as much as I do,
Then I won't stop your marriage, farewell, love, adieu.

Oh Molly, lovely Molly, despite all your charms,
There is many's a night you have lay in my arms.
But if ever I'll return again it'll be in the Spring
Where the mavis and the turtle dove and the nightingale sing.

'Lovely Molly', like 'Sweet Lemeney', is one of many songs in which the nightingale appears in the company of other birds, but still holds this particular sense of principality. The nightingale's placement is often at the melodic and narrative crux of the song. Emotionally, the bird shines brightest as the symbol of nature's enchantment at a moment in a season's (or character's) sexual arising. Transmitted through these songs is a familiarity and awareness that these old singers have of their relationship with the magic of nature and the exquisiteness and potency of the land. These songs communicate a sense of yearning: for our sweethearts, for our homeland and for the birds that sing for us in spring and leave us at the end of summer.

Berkeley Square

It's impossible to know whether, if we were to go back a couple of centuries, we would in fact hear nightingales singing in Mayfair. The birds manage to live quite comfortably today in Berlin's city-centre Tiergarten; and Keats, of course, heard his nightingale in his

London garden in Hampstead. But it has been many years since a nightingale has truly sung in Berkeley Square. However, there is no place in the world more associated with the bird than this rather opulent address.

The song, written in 1939, was a hugely popular wartime ballad for Vera Lynn and a plethora of Americans. It was actually written in a French fishing village by an English entertainer called Eric Maschwitz and the American composer Manning Sherwin. Of course the song makes clear that on those 'certain nights' when lovers meet, anything could happen.

For many years I was determined to get the nightingale back into Berkeley Square – in some sense, at least. I'd investigated this with Westminster Council, only to be told that the hire of the square for a night cost upwards of £15,000, which was outside my budget. However, when in spring 2019 there was a call by Extinction Rebellion for the public to organise actions, it dawned on me that the best model of operation was far simpler. Turning up at a desired space and claiming it as one's arena, as long as it conformed to XR principles and the campaigning agenda of being peaceful and non-violent, was the obvious way to realise my dream. This was not just an ideal way of bringing nightingales back to the square, but – coupled with the movement's central theme of the loss of species – offered a perfect opportunity to celebrate the bird and raise awareness of the nightingales' shocking plight in the UK.

The date of 29 April was chosen, and happened to fall at the end of that month's now-historic first set of mass climate actions. The event, devised and posted on the XR website, inadvertently served as the most perfect closing ceremony for the 'Spring Uprising'. Between XR, my events company (the Nest Collective) and myself, we put out an open invitation to people to help us 'rewild' Berkeley Square, in a most romantic finale to the birthing of this new rebel community. A pop-up flash mob for nature lovers landed in the square, with about 1,500 supporters in all coming together: poets, musicians, activists and curious members of the public alike. Readings, speeches and performances were shared. We played the RSPB's brand-new pure-birdsong single 'Let Nature Sing'. This two-and-a-half-minute track, made up of twenty endangered native birds' song, was something I had composed some months before; the following week it landed in the top twenty in the charts. The street artist ATM even brought along for display a painted nightingale on the tail of an original Wellington bomber, in honour of Beatrice Harrison.

At the appointed hour, everyone began streaming the nightingale's song on their phones. The sound filled the square in glorious tumult, as a huge variety of different nightingales sang out. To accompany this music in full glorious unison, in an updated rendition that I had written for the event, we all joined our voices for 'A Nightingale Sang in Berkeley Square':

> How strong we are, like never before
> We're here because we care
> But those hazy crazy nights we met
> And dreamed nightingales sang in Berkeley Square ...

This was a reimagining of the song, with the possibility that we could change the world; that we could even make a nightingale sing in Berkeley Square. The massive ancient plane trees in the square rang with music, banners and song. As darkness fell and we ceremoniously closed the gathering at 9.30 p.m. (just as I'd promised the very forgiving park keeper), everyone slowly drifted away, still streaming the birdsong as they left the park. As people wandered across London back to their homes on foot, by bike, bus and Tube, I'm told the birdsong continued, as people defiantly let their phones sing our nightingale's song for as long as they possibly could.

LUSCINIA PHILOMELA.

Walter. Imp.

CHAPTER EIGHT

FOLKSONG AND ARTSONG: SINGING WITH NIGHTINGALES AROUND THE WORLD

The most memorable encounters with nature sometimes come at times and in ways you least expect. In 2010 I wasn't quite on the path to being a fully fledged nightingale obsessive and had no idea of the international reach of this bird. I was unenlightened about the nightingale's abundance in mainland Europe, and in the folklore and song traditions of each country. It was only a few years after my first pilgrimage to Arlington Reservoir, and that year the nightingales had passed me by, evading my naive attempts to find them. Somehow I had managed to hear them every spring except this one. I thought I could simply turn up in places that felt nightingale-friendly and – just like a blackbird or song thrush – a nightingale would probably spark up. If I'd known how sparsely nightingales are found, I would probably not have tried as hard as I did that year. That June I'd been invited to teach in Croatia on a residential music course in a small, medieval hilltop town called Grožnjan, and my fortunes were about to change.

Grožnjan is built on a conical mountain plateau. It is tiny, fortressed, and famous for its many art studios and galleries. This extraordinary labyrinthine walled town, with cascading vineyards all around, pro-trudes out of the high plateau looming over the valley below. I was lucky enough to be there for a saint's holiday, an annual celebration for the town, and was told that all the villagers would gather in the central square to celebrate as the sun set.

After a long day of teaching and dinner with the students, I began my search for the square, to find a sparse number of gathered towns-folk being entertained by a one-man band with a Casio keyboard, who played a set of 1990s Europop tunes with a backing band provided with a full set of synth-demo sounds. This was not what I had envisaged. To escape, I quietly slipped away, hoping to find some silence, but the acoustics of the stone citadel meant that everywhere I went, I was chased from behind by the digital 'oompah' drum machine. I headed to the town's only entrance and exit, the portcullis gate, and onto the dusty road beyond.

Outside I was greeted by the piny, bitumen scent of a long row of tall cypress trees, which led the eye up to the hill's crest far ahead. They guarded a high-walled cemetery, alongside which I walked to escape the wafting sounds of tinny pop. I followed the road higher. The town's floodlights receded and my eyes softened to the dark night. I walked further still, now through olive groves whose ghostly gnarled limbs inhaled the town's noises and exhaled a rich silence. Finally a new sound tinged the air. Familiar whistles and squeals came from the distance. I initially wondered, as I often do when first hearing the far-off song of the nightingale, if the sound might actually be the swish of my trousers as I moved – distorted harmonic whispers. I climbed higher and higher, and the sounds grew louder and louder until the olives ended, and there ahead of me was a wild expanse: no formal, orderly tree lines, just scrub – rugged, messy and profuse. It was alive with nightingales launching their night-singing. There must have been dozens of them. I had never experienced birdsong like this, let alone with the often-solitary nightingale.

I followed deeper into this impenetrable bush until I heard the sound of a singer right above me. It seemed I had found my own gallery of saints for this holy day, and here was the most wonderful invitation to practise some self-directed holy communion with this avian liturgy. For hours I journeyed on the wings of these brown-feathered vessels, ricocheting from bird to bird across this wondrous nightscape. The birds had risen into full song that rippled out of the trees, with the glow of the city beyond.

A Croatian coin featuring a nightingale

Eventually I retreated gently back through the olive groves, with the nightingales in slow diminuendo. As I returned to the town, my ears caught the trails of something new – something equally otherworldly. The pop music had finished and now, emerging from the town, was a familiar, yet equally ancient humming sound. I stopped and held my breath. There I stood, 200 metres from the town, on the threshold between two of the greatest sound-worlds I might ever hear: behind me was the rapturous banter of male nightingales, and ahead of me the drones and chantings of men in polyphonic song. For a few moments I stood in wonder at the singularity of all this music – at the thousands of years of tradition before me and behind me.

Local expressions

The nightingale and his song have appeared in the poetry and prose, mythology and music passed down by people across the Northern Hemisphere for thousands of years. This fleeting visitor, a bird that sings for just a few short weeks of the year, is known across the world through inherent, localised symbolism, demonstrating strong bonds with those who lived and worked close to the bird. They prompt a diversity of expressions, from the poetry and devotional song of Turkey to the ribaldry of the English folk tradition.

On a recording trip with the BBC in 2018 I recorded nightingale imitations played in the shepherds' music of the Epirus mountains in northern Greece, with tunes known as *skaros*. Historically, in the months when the nightingale wasn't singing, in a land full of sheep-hungry wolves, these songs helped to calm the shepherd's flock. The *skaros*, first played on simple reed or bird-boned flutes and later transferred to violins and clarinets, now survive through the village festivals of dance and feasting known as *panegyria*, which create a calming, yet ecstatic state of trance for the community to dance to.

A little further east, the Afghan people's reverence and adoration for the nightingale is endemic. In this culture, birds and birdsong are venerated as symbols of religious music and prayer, and as the voice of God. Their music is viewed as another form of *zikr*, a Sufi practice in which adherents come together to perform recitations and prayers accompanied by ritualistic breathing and body movements. The birds are believed to be intoning the Names of God to the heavens.

In Afghanistan, canaries, nightingales and caged singing birds were brought to musical gatherings and encouraged to participate. Their song was used as a form of music in itself. John Baily, Emeritus

Professor of Ethnomusicology at Goldsmiths University, London, spent many years conducting research into native music in Afghanistan and observed musicians bringing caged birds to recordings, like just another instrument. He describes the master players of the *rubab* (a small lute-like instrument in the *tar* family of instruments) telling of sitting at night beneath the mulberry or fig trees and calling down the nightingales with their playing. The birds would perch upon the tuning pegs and would chorus with the music.

The song of the nightingale represents a heavenly voice in Persian music and poetry. Known there as *bulbul*, this is the bird of *hazaâr dastân* – 'a thousand stories'. Along with the rose, the nightingale is the central symbol of love and loss:

> Everyone who has read Persian, if only in translation, knows of the nightingale who yearns for the rose – it is, in mystical language, the soul longing for eternal beauty … The nightingale infinitely repeats the praise of the rose without tiring, tells of its longing, sings hymns from the Koran of the rose (i.e., its petals), suffers without complaint the stings of the thorns. [The poet] Iqbal has interpreted the song of the nightingale in the context of his philosophy of unfulfilled union and longing – only longing gives the soul bird the capacity to sing, inspiring it to create lovely melodies. Longing is the highest state the soul can reach, for it results in creativity, whereas union brings about silence and annihilation.[5]

The nightingale is often said to be so in love with the rose that he presses his breast against the thorn, so that the blood runs out, to turn the white rose red.

---

[5] Annemarie Schimmel, *Mystical Dimensions of Islam* (Chapel Hill: University of North Carolina Press, 1975).

NIGHTINGALES.—*Luscinia vera* and *Luscinia philomela*.

There are many Turkish folk songs and lamentations, such as the traditional *Bülbülüm Altın Kafeste* ('My Nightingale in a Golden Cage') and *Seherde Ağlayan Bülbül* ('The Crying Nightingale'). And some wonderfully poetic lyrics of the *bülbül* can be found in the *Bülbül Kaside* ('Song of the Nightingale"):

> Is the Father's name your mantra?
> Are those gardens your home?
> Is your plight just as mine?
> Don't sing in sorrow, nightingale,
> I see you feel for the rose.
> Who'd know of the rose?
> Seating around the rose bush are you

Whispering your song to the budding rose?
I know you fell for the green,
Quietly turned to worldly gains I see.
Don't add to this issue in my head,
My sweet nightingale.

Across in India, the nightingale has a similar relationship in the songs of peasant singers and their close relationship with the natural world. In the northern states of Kashmir and the higher snow-covered Himalayas birds abound, with kingfishers, paradise flycatchers, hoopoes, nightingales and golden orioles. There the popular folk song entitled simply 'Song of the Nightingale' is woven into the Hindu rhythmic musical system knows as *raga*, accompanied by a bamboo flute and a *sarangi* string instrument. On the south coast, in Kerala, you might find an instrument called the *BulBul* – literally 'the nightingale' – which is a little zither (a stringed instrument) with a keyboard. The *BulBul* was played by the Pullavans, a caste employed in medicine and midwifery who used incantations and sorcery within their *Sarpam Pattu* (Serpent Song) dancing rituals, held within the snake-groves and sung as fertility rites.

The song of lovers

As the birds appear across Central Asia, meeting the Silk Road from the east, the nightingale features repeatedly in poetry, but also in music. In Kyrgyzstan a solo instrumental genre known as *kuu* is part of a nomadic musical tradition that captures a sound-portrait of the nightingale's uncommon song, in a manner that is wonderfully intricate and descriptive. Musicians such as Ruslan Jumabaev, player of the lute-like *komuz*, have recorded *Bulbul Sayrak* ('Singing Nightingale') and captured the bird's song with a localised quality that we know so well, but with shades of the high tundra in it and the sparse instrumental styles of the steppe.

There is a similarly rich seam of nightingale-influenced music a short flight further north in Russia, where the romanticising of the nightingale feels particularly developed. Here, the bird appears as a character and a witness in lovers' songs, and loses that more ancient embodied quality. Russian Gypsy songs embrace the nightingale in the human domain as the bird of love and loss, as opposed to the nightingale portraits in Eastern European and Central Asian music, which take humans into the bird's world:

The Nightingales *(Solovyi)*

Nightingales, nightingales,
Don't disturb the soldiers,
Let the soldiers sleep awhile.

Spring came to the front,
The lads cannot sleep
Not because of the cannonade,
But because the crazy nightingales,
Paying no attention to the battles,
Sing again all night long.

What does a nightingale care about war?
The nightingale has its own life.
The sleepless soldier remembers a house,
A green garden with a pond

Where the nightingales sing all night long,
And in this house someone awaits the soldier.[6]

The bird that brought joy

The nightingale is the national bird of Ukraine, and an old folk saying there says that it can understand Ukrainian, because it is such a lyrical and melodic language. Stories tell that the nightingale once lived only in India, and would fly around the world collecting songs for the Emperor. One day the nightingale came to Ukraine and was so deeply saddened by the country's sorrowful music that he opened his mouth and gave forth his strident, uplifting song to fill the people with happiness. Ever since, he visits each springtime to listen and join the joyful music of the people.

This story is sometimes inverted to relate that the Indian visitor found Ukrainian music so happy that he insisted on visiting each year to sing with, and hear, the beautiful song. Certainly the bird is a potent symbol of spring and new life, and of love and beauty. *Soloveiko* (nightingale) is used as a Ukrainian term of endearment. 'Even the memory of the nightingale's song makes man happy,' said Taras Shevchenko, the renowned Ukrainian poet.

Further south-west in Serbia the field recordings of Dragoslav Dević feature a unique example of the singer Novica Jeftić presenting 'how a swarm of bees is being decoyed to the beehive' through bird impersonation calls. The song entitled '*Mat, mat . . . kuti bubo*' is undoubtedly a nightingale (*slavuj* in Serbian) rendered by means of the human voice and whistle.

[6] From Yulya, *Yulya sings Russian Gypsy Songs*, (New York : Moniter Records, 1966)

The river of woe

Across Europe, folk songs tell of the nightingale in all his guises. In the north-western corner of Greece, in the Black Mountains of Epirus, you will find the River Acheron. In Greek mythology this was the 'River of Woe' across which the ferryman Charon transported departed souls to enter the Greek Underworld, Hades. Ancient music comes from these lands and is believed to be some of the oldest folk music in Europe; and the nightingale sings proudly from within some of the most heartbreaking songs upon this Earth.

Epirean music is discordant, to most Western ears – reflecting the darkness of the mountains, the deep valleys and gorges. But in Greece it is far more than mere entertainment or symbolism; it takes on a deeply spiritual function, to connect the people to the land beneath their feet, and especially to channel the state of *xenitea*: the sense of loss or separation from a distant home. *Xenitea* is an emotional quality, highly revered and defining the Greek state of mind, and is an expression commonly recognised within the nightingale's song by musicians and artists there.

We also hear the nightingale in wondrous depiction, recorded in the 1920s and later, in iso-polyphonic music – which connects to Byzantine traditional church music, where group singing is accompanied by a choral 'drone' part. The *birbilio* (Greek dialect for 'nightingale', and also a region in Greece) literally weeps in *Stis Deropolis Ton Kampo* ('On the Deropolis Plain'). This song encompasses Albanian, Turkish, northern Greek and the Sephardic Hebrew of Thessaloniki among its influences. The moaning lament simply drips with a sense of loss and woe:

> On the Deropolis plain (nightingale weeping)
> Young Yannis lies on the ground (nightingale weeping),

He had his horse tethered (nightingale weeping).

'Rise, master, ride again' (nightingale weeping).

'I can't, poor Grivas[7] (nightingale weeping),

Love has left me wounded.'

Across the border in Albania (where the iso-polyphonic tradition is also strong) you can hear the popular *Ja thoshte bilbili* ('Sang the Nightingale'), another song of lost love:

Sang the nightingale,

I opened up the window.

My wits have fled me,

Fled to my mistress.

Sang the nightingale

At the castle gate,

Ah sad, oh sorrowful,

no harm befall thee.

This eve the maid departed

Left us all alone.

Sang the nightingale

From quince tree to quince tree.

I laid my head down and I slept

Upon thy breast.[8]

However, the pinnacle of all sound recordings of European music depicting the nightingale has to be the iconic 1929 violin rendition of

---

[7] Listen to the wonderful *Lament from Epirus* by Various Artists, Orange Amaro 2019

[8] There is a wonderful album *Early Albanian Traditional Songs & Improvisations, 1920s–1930s* by Various Artists, Orange Amaro 2019

Selfos ('Nightingale') by Demitrios Halkias, a Greek Roma master who recorded with the clarinettists Kitsos Harisiadis and Manthos Halkias and other great musicians of the era. The folklorist and record collector Christopher King says of *Selfos*:

> This instrumental is essentially a dance piece that mimics the song of the nightingale and serves as a showcase for the violinist's command of the high registers, harmonics and avian mimicry on the instrument. It also illuminates one of the mysterious techniques of Epirotic musicians: their ability to explore the tonal possibilities of a scale while increasing the dramatic tension of the piece. Halkias does this almost effortlessly. His obsession with a given phrase comes to rest on a note not necessarily in that scale but that amplifies the expectation of the listener. And then he relaxes the tension. Epirotic musicians were masters of this technique of emotional 'catch and release'.[9]

King could be speaking of the nightingale himself here, and when you hear this recording, and many other recordings that imitate the nightingale, you realise how influential the bird has been in this musical field.

Tales of love and loss

In Czechoslovakia and Moravia the nightingale again features as a motif and representation for love, and often as a messenger, too. The nightingale often delivers a note of love, or appears at the opening of a song before lovers meet. These songs are written in dialect: the

[9] From Christopher King, *Lament from Epins* by Various Artists, Orange Amaro 2019

Czech term for the nightingale is *slavík*, but you will often find the diminutive form *slavíček* in Czech lyrics, as is typical in Czech folk songs. Below are three folk-song tableaux portraying the bird entwined with love and loss:

> The nightingale sings,
> The grove resonates.
> The one without a lover
> Should look for her.

> I don't have a lover,
> I will not look for her.
> I will rather go
> Right away in the army.[10]

★

> The nightingale is a little bird.
> Yes, it would reach high,
> It flew up high
> On a dry fir tree.
> It flew up, sat down and sang a song.
> Tell me, my love, my dear one,
> Yes, to whom your folks will give you?
> They have brought me up for you,
> [but] They did not allow me to want you.
> Yes, because you do not own any field.[11]

★

[10] From the village of Velká nad Veličkou, Czech Republic, 1925.
[11] From the village of Horní Bečva, Czech Republic, 1908.

> The nightingale is a little bird, it flies high
> Over the mountains and valleys, singing sweet.
> It will sing at midnight
> When my sweetheart goes to bed
> When she dreams about me in her sleep.[12]

In Spain there is a beautiful Jewish Sephardic song about the *bilbilicos* (*ruiseñores* in Spanish) called *Los Bilbilicos Cantan*, which would traditionally have been sung by women. The name *bilbilicos* comes from the Turkish, which, after their exile eastwards, provided many words to the Judaeo-Spanish language of the Sephardic people who settled in the Ottoman Empire. The following song is a *cantiga* – a Galician-Portuguese medieval-style poem centred on devotion and love – and is believed to have come from the island of Rhodes. There are hundreds of versions of the song across the region, in Greece, Turkey and Bulgaria, which is about the grief of unrequited love. Note the symbolism of the rose again.

The Rose Flowers

> The rose blooms in May,
> My soul darkens, suffering from love,
> Suffering from love.
>
> Nightingales sing, sighing of love
> And the passion kills me, my pain increases,
> My pain increases.

---

[12] From Jan Poláček, *Slovácké pěsničky* (*Folk Songs of the Slovácko Region*), vol. IV (Prague, 1950).

Come more quickly, my dove,

More quickly to me,

More quickly, you my soul, because I feel myself dying,

I feel myself

Dying.

The rose blooms in May,

My soul darkens, suffering from love,

Suffering from love,

Suffering from love.

The German folk tradition was interrupted, and partially erased, by the devastation of the twentieth-century conflict, resulting in a great silencing of the *Volksmusik* or people's music. The traditional song *Nachtigall, ich hör dich singen*, or 'Nightingale, I Hear You Sing', features in the book called *Der Zupfgeigenhansl* (meaning 'the boy who plucks the guitar'). This songbook was published in 1913 by the so-called *Wandervogel* (literally 'migratory / wandering bird'), which was a hugely popular idealist German youth movement that fostered a highly romantic and idealistic back-to-nature response to growing industrialisation. (The Israeli kibbutz vision took its roots from this movement.) It encouraged young people to go hiking and enjoy outdoor pursuits, and the songbook was rich in German traditional folk music and fairy tales. Sadly, what began as a relatively apolitical movement was extinguished by the rise of the Hitler Youth, although many members of the *Wandervogel* aligned themselves to the *Widerstand* (German resistance to Nazism).

The first verse of this song presents a complex moral question, which it is powerful to think of, in the context of the time:

Nightingale, I hear you sing,
The heart'd shatter me in the womb,
Come now, and tell me soon,
How should I conduct myself?

Nightingale, I see you running,
At the brook you do drink,
You dip your little spout,
Like it would be the best wine.

Nightingale, where's a good place to live?
In the linden trees, in the crowns?
At the beautiful Mrs Nightingale's house,
Say hello to my beloved a thousand times.

In France a more rudimentary depiction of the *rossignol* appears in the beautiful lullaby *Bonsoir*, which is profoundly simple and yet meditative, despite its childlike simplicity. I often sing this in French at the nightingale gatherings. It is a short rhyme that, when sung in rotation, has an incredible trance-like effect. The scene described in the lyrics visually renders the very breath of the land:

Bonsoir/Good Evening

Bonsoir, bonsoir,	Good evening, good evening,
Le brume monte du sol.	The mist rises from the ground.
On entend le rossignol,	Listen to the nightingale,
Le brume monte du sol.	The mist rises from the ground.
On entend le rossignol,	Listen to the nightingale,
Bonsoir, bonsoir.	Good evening, good evening.

You may also know *La Claire Fontaine* ('By the Clear Fountain'), another much-loved traditional French song from the 1600s, featuring the nightingale and the rose together once again. Here *fontaine* refers to a spring, and the 'bouquet of roses' represents maidenhood:

> By the clear fountain,
> On my promenade
> I found the water so fair
> That I stopped there to bathe.
> I have loved you for a long, long time,
> Never will I forget you.
>
> Under an oak tree
> I dried myself
> On its highest branch.
> A nightingale was singing,
> I have loved you for a long, long time,
> Never will I forget you.
>
> Sing, nightingale, sing,
> You with your carefree heart.
> Your heart feels like laughing,
> Mine feels like weeping.
> I have loved you for a long, long time,
> Never will I forget you.
>
> I have lost my dear friend
> Without just cause
> For a bouquet of roses

That I refused her.
I have loved her for a long, long time,
Never will I forget her.

I would that the rose
Were still on its briar
And that my sweet friend
Still there to love me.
I have loved her for a long, long time,
Never will I forget her.

I have loved you for a long, long time,
Never ever will I forget you.

Le Rossignol de France.

One of the most widely published music books in Canada is *Chansons populaires du Canada*, first printed in 1865. *Le rossignol* features heavily in traditional French tunes that arrived in the 1600s and remained staples in traditional song. Titles include *J'ai cueilli la belle rose*, *Rossignolet du bois* / 'I picked the beautiful rose', *Rossignol du vert bocage* and *Au bois du rossignolet*, which are translated variously as 'Nightingale of the Woods', 'Nightingale of the Green Woods' and 'In the Wood of the Nightingale'. There were several hundred years of singing about the bird without ever actually hearing one.

Marius Barbeau, one of Canada's great ethnomusicologists and folklorists, worked tirelessly to document traditional French-Canadian and Pacific Northwest First Nation songs and stories. Towards the end of his life he presented a series on Radio-Canada called *Le Rossignol y chante* and wrote a book under the same title. Barbeau spoke of the nightingale as *oiseau messager d'amour* – 'messenger bird of love'. Here are a few of the deeply passionate lines from his collected songs:

> *Rossignolet des bois, rossignolet sauvage,*
> *Apprends-moi ton langage, apprends moi à parler,*
> *Apprends-moi la manière qu'il faut pour aimer.*

> Nightingale, wild nightingale,
> Teach me your language, teach me to speak,
> Teach me the way it takes to love.

★

> *Rossignolet sauvage, le roi des amoureux,*
> *Toi qui vas au village, tu vas voir ses beaux yeux.*

> Wild nightingale, the king of lovers,
>
> You who go to the village, you will see his beautiful eyes.

But for those travellers among you wishing to guarantee hearing a nightingale song (the 'thrush nightingale' as opposed to the 'common') at any time of year, there is one reliable place where his song can be heard, twenty-four hours a day, seven days a week. The toilet facilities of Helsinki airport have been fitted with piped birdsong, and I'm thrilled to say that the lead singer is our nightingale – which just goes to show that cleanliness is indeed next to godliness.

Recording birdsong

Birdsong played a pivotal role in the advancement of sound recording, and the commercial recording industry helped to bring birdsong into our lives as readily as it did into that of professional music-makers. It was the sound-recordist pioneer Ludwig Koch (1881–1974) who seems to have been the first person to make a sound recording of birdsong in 1889. He grew up in Germany and was just eight years old when his parents bought him a phonograph, an early sound-recording device. He was passionate about animals, so he experimented with recording their sounds from an early age. He later worked in the gramophone industry and, after the Second World War, ended up in London, where his experience brought him to the attention of the BBC. It purchased his nature recordings, which became the foundations of the BBC's audio library of natural history. Koch's voice, which accompanied his prominent sound recordings, became well known in the UK on his radio broadcasts. In his autobiography there is even an account of Koch taking the Queen of Belgium and her sister-in-law, the Duchess of Bavaria, with torches in hand, out to record the nightingale.

Whistling

In the US, far from the reach of the nightingale, imitation birdsong became a phenomenon at the height of vaudeville in the eighteenth and early nineteenth centuries. This sparked a market for gramophone recordings of famous 'whistlers'. There was even a school for artistic whistling in California. Marion Darlington is probably the most widely heard, yet unknown product of the school, as the uncredited lips behind the whistles in all the Disney films, including *Cinderella*, *Bambi*, *Pinocchio*, and the lead in the most famous whistling song ever: 'Whistle While You Work' in *Snow White and the Seven Dwarfs*.

Whistling was seen as an art form associated with African-American minstrelsy and the so-called 'Coon' shows of the time. It had a reputation of being the behaviour of wild folk and the unrefined. However, whistling was a part of many people's daily soundworld for generations, and music-hall attendees would the next day recount their recall of entire concerts in pure whistles. Despite this, performers like Al Jolson and George W. Johnson used their routines derogatively to depict the 'whistling coon' image of the nice, but simple African-American. They were partly responsible for the racial stereotyping of whistling and for relegating it to 'primitive' Black entertainment. Due to the physiological production of simply 'putting your lips together and blowing', whistling couldn't be racially or gender-distinguished, which made it a democratically powerful and therefore very dangerous act of expression in a white, male-controlled culture. The degradation and suppression of whistling as a musical art form was therefore inevitable.

The most popular nature 'whistler' was the self-trained Charles Kellogg, who was born in 1868 in Nevada. During his lonely childhood, in which he was raised largely by Native Americans, he learned to emulate a range of animals and birds. He claimed that he was born, like birds, with a syrinx or vocal organ that enabled him to produce two notes at once and thus his performance was actual singing, not whistling – a 'reproduction' of birdsong rather than an 'imitation'.

Kellogg toured the US for fifty years, performing in front of a backdrop of the woods and speaking passionately about his connection with nature. A big break in 1910 made him a star and he became the richest and most famous recording artist in the world at the time. He disliked the terminology 'whistler' for numerous reasons, despite this being a practice with a great connection to our ancient relationship to the bird world.

The sad demise and extinguishing of this exquisite, expressive art form cut another thread connecting us to our 'animal and human' conversational past. The last few legendary masters of bird impersonation slowly passed on, the last of whom was the UK's own Percy Edwards. His love for nature and keen interest in ornithology brought him to prominence after the Second World War. He went on to forge a fascinating TV and film career – famous as the reindeer in *Santa Claus: The Movie* and the eponymous Alien in the film. It is said that Edwards could impersonate up to 600 different birds, but sadly the only footage of his skill is a 1972 cameo on the *Morecambe and Wise Show*, presenting Edwards as a *Britain's Got Talent*-style elderly statesman. The poetic and noble accomplishment of whistling, which requires hours of appreciative listening and study, was by now nothing but a prime-time TV curiosity.

There are, however, reassuring tales of its survival, such as *ku dili*, the Turkish bird language, which is listed by UNESCO as an intangible cultural heritage. There are 10,000 whistlers living in and around Kuşköy, the 'Village of the Birds' in Turkey's northern Pontic Mountains. They communicate across their valleys in a developed series of melodies and whistles. And this same form of communication lives on in communities in New Guinea and the village of Kongthong in India; among the Nepalese Chepang people; in native languages such as Yoruba and Ewe in West Africa; in the Canary Islands and the Pyrenees; among the Mazatec and Chinantec peoples of Mexico's Oaxaca; and in the Amazonas state of Brazil, among the indigenous speakers of Múra-Pirahã.

The orchestra

Nightingale song is unique in being an inspiration not only for sound recordists, stage stars, folk musicians and poets, but also for the great classical composers. In Europe and further afield, many of the great composers have tried to emulate, re-create or extol the majesty of the nightingale's song using human instruments.

George Frederick Handel (1685–1759) – who spent most of his life in England and became a British citizen in 1727 – composed the English oratorio *L'Allegro, il Penseroso ed il Moderato* ('The Joyful, the Contemplative and the Moderate Man') in 1740, based on the quintessentially English poetry of John Milton. He attempted to re-create a picture of the English pastoral idyll, and so of course the 'Philomel' (a name oft used in the classics for the nightingale, see page 176) must appear amid the ploughman, the milkmaid, the mower and 'hillocks green':

> Less Philomel will deign a song,
> In her sweetest, saddest plight,
> Smoothing the rugged brow of night.
>
> Sweet bird, that shun'st the noise of folly,
> Most musical, most melancholy!
> Thee, chauntress, oft the woods among,
> I woo to hear thy even-song.
> Or, missing thee, I walk unseen,
> On the dry smooth-shaven green,
> To behold the wand'ring moon
> Riding near her highest noon.
> Sweet bird ...

PHILOMEL · AND · PROGNE.

A few years later Handel included the Nightingale Chorus in his English oratorio *Solomon* (best known for 'The Arrival of the Queen of Sheba'). Here, an exquisite chorus of nightingales (represented by flutes) show Solomon's love for his queen in the cedar grove. And one of Handel's best-known orchestral pieces is his Organ Concerto No. 13, which has the nickname 'The Cuckoo and the Nightingale' for its wonderful characterisations of these two birds in dialogue. These two springtime proclaimers provide popular challenges for the composer to replicate, and the nightingale features in compositions and operas from Biber, Mendelssohn, Liszt, Grieg, Stravinsky, Ravel and others. Beethoven's 'Pastoral Symphony' ticks off the cuckoo, the trills of the nightingale and the rhythmic quail; and Vivaldi's *Four Seasons* includes the nightingale in the summer chorus, along with the cuckoo and the turtle dove.

In the modern era the Italian composer Ottorino Respighi (1879–1936) brought nature into the concert hall. His small orchestral suite *Gli uccelli* ('The Birds') featured five movements inspired by Renaissance, baroque and early-music attempts at re-creating birdsong. *L'usignuolo* ('The Nightingale'), the fourth suite, was actually based on Jacob van Eyck's recorder transpositions of the folk song *Engels Nachtegaeltje* ('The English Nightingale').

In 1924 Respighi's larger-scale 'Pines of Rome', the second of his trilogy of orchestral poems of Rome, described the pine trees of the city over the course of a day. At the end of the third movement, a nocturne set under the full moon, the instructions are for the orchestra to be silent and for a 78-rpm phonograph recording of a nightingale to play. Respighi even stipulated that a bird recorded in Rome be used. Could his choice of a nightingale recorded in Rome be in homage to John Keats, the great nightingale poet, who died in Rome in 1821? This was the first use of mixed media in classical music, and took place the same year as Beatrice Harrison's live broadcast. It seems that 1924 was a good year for nightingales.

The French composer Olivier Messiaen (1908–92) found his connection to birdsong when he became a prisoner of war in the spring of 1940. While captured, he wrote his most important piece, *Quatuor pour la fin du temps* ('Quartet for the End of Time'), which begins with a clarinet-blackbird singing and a violin-nightingale improvisation. Messiaen was devoted to birdsong and a fanatical ornithologist, who was obsessed with hearing as many species singing in the wild as possible. He spent hours in his garden and further afield, making scientific notations of their music in his notebooks. Wonderful records remain of the visualisation and staff-notation of his encounters, and especially rich are his graphite snatches of *'Rossignol'* across the pages. All of his later pieces included birdsong in some way. His *Réveil des oiseaux* ('Dawn Chorus'/'The Awakening of the Birds') is Messiaen's collection of thirty-eight different birds as they appear from 12 a.m. right through the night to the dawn chorus, and then on to the morning singers. The piece begins and ends, of course, with the nightingale.

To conclude this grand world tour, which highlights only a fraction of the many times that nightingales dazzle in their range of charismatic identities, I want to mention the *Chunaengjeon* or 'Dance of Spring Nightingale'. This Korean court-dance from the Joseon Dynasty (1392–1897), when Korea was ruled by China, appeared when the Emperor Gaozong heard the nightingale singing and ordered his court musician Po Ming Chien to re-interpret the song in a musical composition. A small mat was provided, and a female dancer performed on it in a bird-like fashion, moving back and forth and turning around. The song text translates as: 'Walking in the moonlight, wind through sleeves, standing before a flower, yearning for a lover.' Although hard to pinpoint what aspects of the bird's song or indeed movements have influenced this performance, it certainly has an exuberant yet harmful tone and the dance is still performed today.

The nightingale around the world

European language	Name for the nightingale
Albanian	*bilbil*
Basque	*ruiseñor*
Belarusian	*салавей*
Bosnian	*slavuj*
Bulgarian	*славей*
Catalan	*rossinyol*
Croatian	*slavuj*
Czech	*slavík*
Danish	*nattergal*
Dutch	*nachtegaal*
Estonian	*ööbik*
Finnish	*satakieli*
French	*rossignol*
Galician	*rousinol*
German	*Nachtigall*
Greek	*αηδόνι (aidóni)*
Hungarian	*csalogány*
Icelandic	*næturgali*
Irish	*filiméala*
Italian	*usignolo*
Latvian	*lakstīgala*
Lithuanian	*lakštingala*
Macedonian	*славеј*
Maltese	*rożinjol*
Norwegian	*nattergal*
Polish	*słowik*
Portuguese	*rouxinol*
Romanian	*privighetoare*
Russian	*соловей (solovey)*
Serbian	*славуј (slavuj)*
Slovak	*slávik*

Slovenian	*slavček*
Spanish	*ruiseñor*
Swedish	*näktergal*
Turkish	*bülbül*
Ukrainian	соловей (*solovey*)
Welsh	*eos*
Yiddish	סאָלאָוויי

Asian language	Name for the nightingale
Armenian	սոխակ
Azerbaijani	*bülbül*
Bengali	পাপিয়া
Chinese Simplified	夜莺 (*yèyīng*)
Chinese Traditional	夜鶯 (*yèyīng*)
Georgian	ბულბული
Gujarati	બુલબુલ
Hindi	बुलबुल
Japanese	ナイチンゲール
Kannada	ನೈಟಿಂಗೇಲ್
Kazakh	бұлбұл
Korean	나이팅게일 (*naiting-geil*)
Lao	nightingale
Malayalam	രാപ്പാടി
Marathi	नाइटगील
Nepali	बुलबुल
Sinhala	බුරුමියට
Tamil	அந்தக்குயில்
Telugu	నైటింగేల్
Thai	นกไนติงเกล
Urdu	بلبل
Uzbek	*bulbul*
Vietnamese	*Chim đêm*

CHAPTER NINE

BLACKTHORN BLUES: RIDDLE OF THE SYRINX

I realise now that trying to describe the nightingale's song, and the experience around it, is akin to retelling one's previous night's dream to the barista making your morning coffee. It doesn't quite translate. It's a sound that can only truly be understood through first-hand experience, and justice is never quite served when attempting to articulate it. To describe in words the complexity of the nightingale's sounds poses a tremendous challenge. Clare, Keats and Milton have already addressed the bird in so many guises with great effect, and so anyone writing about the nightingale has these giants of literature as pillars of interpretation to avoid imitating. But the truth of the challenge lies in the way the nightingale possesses the strange skill of uttering every possible character, tone and temperature imaginable. His song has personality and textural shape all at once. He is the master of the oxymoron, disobeying both time and space.

I could use the following vocabulary to describe the nightingale: mercurial, spacious, gymnastic, brazen, exuberant, melancholic, boastful, piquant, intimate, tender, reticent, garrulous, generous, vulnerable, queer, wistful, wanton, lascivious, brittle, aquiline, digital, pleated, poignant, elegiac, flamboyant, histrionic and wounded. Tomorrow, however, I might choose very different adjectives. I think of the nightingale as an eloquent, feathered, lyrical conversant – the *megarhynchos* thesaurus – with a vocabulary as wide as his bill. I do wonder if the ancient-Greek translation of his Latin name as 'great bill' refers more to his word count and less to the breadth of his gape.

My reluctance to subscribe to any particular definition or classification is purely due to what I see as the nightingale's lyrical prowess. Like the greatest arias and symphonies, his song seems to amplify and return all that his listener brings to the wooded auditorium. To misquote Robert Frost: 'no tears in the bringer, no tears in the singer'. He is the Joni Mitchell of the thicket; the nightingale sings your very truth, undressing and exposing, and not always painting the most flattering portrait of yourself.

Like any blues or jazz musician, the nightingale scorns the daily rhythms of other birds. Many people assume he sings just at night, but his song can be heard intermittently throughout the day, as a taster of his night-show. He remains much quieter during the dawn chorus, and appears only sporadically during the evening chorus.

The day-song is subtly different from the night-song, softer and not as full or continuous, yet also less elegant in its sense of space and phrasing, less dexterous even. This can be difficult to judge, though, when you are listening to him along with a cacophony of other songs, compared to the obliging isolation of the dark and lack of orchestra behind him. As the evening chorus sounds, his day-song ends and he will resume the stage at around 10.30 p.m., varying with the latitude and the season. His start time, like the greatest impresarios, changes every night; and as the nights shorten, so his performance time slips ever later.

Winging it

You have to wonder if the nightingale has any awareness of just how exceptional his music is. Nightingales display an improvised musical style, unlike the fixed style of the wren, for instance, or the turtle dove or robin, which will sing the same phrases over and over again. The nightingale will regale us with around 250 different phrases, and can parade more than 1,500 sounds in total. The deliciously lyrical blackbird, by comparison, has 100 sounds; and the skylark 350 notes. Nightingales have a vast repertoire of musical components, but construct their song from a randomly generated set of phrases. Their song doesn't have determinable patterns, although the nightingale does regularly return to a simple leitmotif – a single phrase specific to individual birds. These leitmotifs are usually a variation on one long fluted note, which can help listeners distinguish one bird from another.

The song is so unfamiliar and rare, however, that inexperienced, enthusiastic bird lovers often mistake other prolific singers for the nightingale, most commonly the city street-light-inspired night-shows of the blackbird, which is one of the only birds that sings roughly within the major key, a joyful song with a throaty and diverse set of phrases. When people I meet share their 'midwinter nightingale encounters', they have often, in fact, met the song of either the robin (also called the 'false nightingale') or the blackbird.

The much-loved robin sings all year round, with a song that for me, even in the middle of spring, offers a frosted reminder of winter never too far away. His bubbling and detailed phrases are too fast for us to

THE NIGHTINGALE.

appreciate fully; he is able to generate vast amounts of musical motifs at exceptional velocity. In response to a January bird-count project, the RSPB said, 'We've had lots of calls from people sharing what they'd spotted during their Big Garden Birdwatch, but many also called rather excitedly to say they'd heard nightingales singing in the evenings. They were a little disappointed when we told them the birds were almost certainly robins, although they were still surprised to find out these birds sing at night.'

The wren's song is also particularly distinctive, with an almost wind-up automaton tone and a strictly set pattern. It's a declarative and combative song that reveals the size-defying brutishness of the wren, the most common of all the songbirds in Britain.

The song thrush also has a wide variety of sounds and, at times, appears to deliver very similar notes to the nightingale. His 'top of the tree' three-repeated-note proclamations have real hints of the nightingale, especially as the song thrush is often the first and last singer to rise and settle for the dawn and dusk choruses. In a territory that hosts both birds, I can, at moments, tell that a song thrush and nightingale have influenced each other, revealing a cross-contamination of styles.

Learned song

The ability of birds to imitate each other – or, indeed, external man-made sounds – is exemplified in the formidable story of 'learned song', as told by the BBC sound recordist Chris Watson. There lives a group of starlings in a bothy on the island of Coll in the Western Isles that has acquired and inherited down the generations the rhythms and sounds of a two-stroke engine. Despite the engine being long out of commission and rusting away, the local starlings' forefathers and -mothers had not only learned to reproduce the sound, but then passed down the generations this faithful interpretation of a long-lost percussive motor. I relish this demonstration of song learning and memory.

The nightingale, upon first hearing him, can be disconcerting in his abstract, midi-like modernity, as if he has been nesting next to a 1990s computer console. When hearing him for the first time each year, I am repeatedly astounded by his tonality and can find him slightly acerbic at first. But I calibrate to the sound and, after a few minutes, wouldn't ask for anything different.

Making music

But how can such a tiny creature produce such a variety of sounds? How does the physiology of this bird achieve so much more than monophonic singers like me could ever dream of doing? It is said that birds sing from the heart. Unlike our single larynx (voice box), birds have a small adapted organ called a syrinx (taken from the Greek for 'pan pipes'), which sits at the base of their trachea (windpipe) in their chest. A bird's syrinx is essentially two separate voice boxes, which are formed where the trachea divides into air sacs. This permits birds to produce simultaneously two singular sounds, and each side of the air sac has its own perfectly distinct vocal skills and techniques. The different sides of the syrinx are often associated with different notes or registers, but you can also recognise when a nightingale is about to hand over a repeating phrase from one air sac to another. It proves to be a rather impressive musical sleight-of-hand.

These dual air sacs also make continuous singing achievable. When, for instance, you hear a skylark produce an almost all-summer-long constant trickle of song, this is the syrinx at work. The nightingale's song is a seamless model of this faculty. He sings with such capacity – there is no way the bird can hold that amount of song, at that notable volume, in his lungs on just one out-breath. The nightingale is able to sing out and take in air at the same time.

But what might nightingales make of their own song? Birds' brains have a much higher processing power than ours, so they experience everything around them far more quickly than humans. It's why they move so fast and respond to environmental changes so speedily. The way we speak and move must appear extraordinarily slow to them. This is revealed most clearly in their ability to sing. Their higher temporal resolution equates to 'frames per second' when shooting a film. When we shoot film, we're working at thirty-five frames per second, whereas birds are seeing the world at roughly fifty frames per second.

This means that the detail birds hear in each other's song is very different from what reaches our ears – plus they have the ability to hear a wider range of sound. We can only fully appreciate this if we take a bird recording and slow it down. If you listen to a slow-speed recording of a wren, robin or nightingale, it reveals a melodic passage that rises and falls dramatically. The song is filled with canyons and valleys and spikes and trills, and whipping, whooping modulations, mordents and split-tone scats. To a musician's ears, even at half-speed, these birds are employing the decorative singing techniques of some of the most gifted professional human singers. The slowed-down sound of the nightingale is quite phenomenal. It reveals impressive detail and technique, and consistency of tonal pitching, all of which is hidden from us within the song, when listened to at a normal rate. Only in slow-motion can we really appreciate what the nightingale hen, searching the night for her partner, will be hearing: far more different music than our sluggish ears can comprehend.

The musician David Rothenberg has uncovered the miraculous similarities that such songs have with the song of the humpback whale, in the whale's low swells and rapid grunts. Not that the birds are hearing each other at that low pitch, but it's fascinating to realise the similarities in their musical expressions.

Master of the night

At the heart of the nightingale's show are timing and setting. It's good to be a singer at night – song travels much further in the damp night air. As the temperature decreases, the air contracts, cools and condenses, leaving dense, moist air, which is ideal for conducting sound. Clearly the nightingale adapts to nature's ever-changing atmosphere; he will usually sing regardless of the rain and blustery weather, though he may hesitate from singing when it is very windy. There are exceptions: some April nights everything might seem to us perfectly calm, even balmy, and yet the nightingales just aren't moved to sing.

The nightingale exploits the acoustics of the night-landscape by singing upwards and outwards in all directions, his noises reflecting off the trees. He will throw his voice from side to side to achieve a superior reach, which, for the non-avian listener, creates disorientation concerning the bird's placement. As he sends the sound out – over here, to the left, to the right, moving around – it becomes more of a struggle to figure out exactly where he is, even if the rest of the forest is silent. As well as showing off and spreading his sonic peacock tail around, so to speak, this disorientation also provides a protective measure, disguising his position from night-hunting birds or ground-hunting animals in search of night-snacks.

You will usually hear the nightingale from afar first, the phrasing becoming stronger and stronger as you approach. At first you hear the subtle squeals of the song – and when you find the birds, you hear the song in its full glory. People often comment on the volume of the nightingale's song, which can be heard more than a mile away when the bird is in full throat. It is said that nightingales were so disturbing to a praying Edward the Confessor that the request went out to clear the local vicinity of the birds, to allow peace in Havering-atte-Bower in Essex. This tale is also sometimes attributed to Thomas à Becket as the nightingale-banisher in Otford, Kent. Whichever one of them it was, I've heard this sentiment shared by sleep-deprived French farmers kept up all night by 'local singers' below their windows.

If you make a habit of listening to nightingales, you will learn to distinguish each voice's character, and to identify the younger from the more mature males. Where denser populations of nightingales exist, one or two younger males will often pipe up earlier – keen to make an impact sooner in the evening perhaps. The older cocks hone their song over time. They learn and practise the sounds they judge to be successful, and tend towards tried-and-tested patterns, focusing their repertoire.

Studies in Germany have shown a significant change in song choices between first- and second-year males. Those in their second breeding season reinvent their repertoire from the previous year, picking up more patterns and similarities with local males, and dropping songs

that were perhaps deemed unsuccessful. They reduce their repertoire by about one-third for the second breeding season, displaying more ordered characteristics or regular patterns in their singing and acoustic structuring. This means they are shaping their song to be more attractive to females, and adapting it to what elicits more positive responses in both male and female nightingales. Thus it is often the younger males that sing a wider range of notes and are louder, and perhaps more brazen and showy, with their music. It seems that the exuberance of youth also exists among nightingales.

The nightingale's true mastery is revealed in the silences between his soundings. These moments of profound suspense are as potent as the song itself. When he opens his beak, thoughts are washed away and the bird rinses right through you, as if you almost become the bird. You dissolve into his song. Then as he stops, your thoughts flood back into that space, into the new silence, as if cleansed, sparkling with a fresh clarity. And repeat. There's a yin and yang between the all-encompassing sounds and the affecting silences.

Often a longer period of silence between phrases indicates that the nightingale is listening for responses from other males, so we have to question how much they are posturing to one another and not just to the females flying above. They can, of course, tell whether the calls they hear are from local males or females that are in the market for a partner.

Studies have shown that the nightingale's trills and buzzes indicate his strength and maturity to the females looking for a mate. Such vocal gymnastics are physically tiring for the male bird, enabling the female to assess swiftly the suitability and substance of a potential partner. Whereas we hear a complex refrain in the bird's song, the hens scouting the area hear an impressive display of stamina and strength. The more complex and challenging songs will likely emanate from a male with greater maturity and vigour. Hence he reveals himself as a strong candidate, probably bearing good genes and chick-rearing skills, to produce healthy nestlings that will grow up able to survive the long journey ahead. Once paired, male nightingales help to feed the females and nestlings, unlike many other types of birds, so these are reasonable attributes for the hens to look for. It's even said that a nightingale can develop a local 'dialect' in his singing, which, in itself, is another signal to the female that this bird has an association with a breeding ground and is therefore probably a survivor.

Groups of nightingales seem to sing in synchronicity in a couple of ways. I have often observed a call-and-response pattern within groups of birds. A *'whiiilllll'* is passed to a neighbour. Then another takes the lead, and so on, in an extraordinary relay. Next, quite unexpectedly, they broadcast simultaneously the same note or phrase at exactly the same moment and in the same key, as if communicating telepathically. I am led to believe that there is more happening than we realise in their minds and in their song – a communal sense of the music that they are tapping into.

Nightingale personalities

The esteemed philosopher, ornithologist, composer and musician David Rothenberg has researched the nightingale's song and written extensively on the behavioural traits and musicality of these birds. His groundbreaking research, working in tandem with Dr Sarah Darwin (see page 44), the great-great-granddaughter of Charles Darwin, is published in a book called *Nightingales in Berlin*. It is wonderful to see such esteemed minds working on solving the mysteries of this special creature. David categorises the males into three different personalities:

1 The Inserter – appears to work with other males in a call-and-response rhythm, inserting his song into the pause when another bird has stopped.

2 The Overlapper – constantly tries to drown out the singing of others by starting his own music just after another bird has begun.

3 The Autonomous Singer – sings regardless of what else is going on around him and doesn't engage with the other males.

In most experiences of listening to multiple birds singing, I have identified all three characters teasing me in the darkness. Doesn't this character assessment work as much for humanity as it does for nightingales?

Old friends

As a bird ages, his song will change, but often a certain feature remains. When returning to a nightingale site that I am familiar with, I will often recognise an old friend's return by a particular slant on a phrase or a certain repeated gesture. Most seasons I will find one or two birds that respond well to music and are particularly cooperative to sing with, and I will continue to play with them for many evenings.

In the first couple of years that I took people out to listen to nightingales in Sussex, there was one bird with particularly distinctive and stunning phrases. I've never heard another bird do quite what he did, improvising and sustaining notes at that level. He had the most extraordinary strength of voice and riffs and would have made the perfect musical partner, had he not chosen a habitat right next to the local sewage-treatment works. No doubt the richness of insect life in the area made this an ideal place for a bird, but it meant he was accompanied by a constant mechanical groan – not the best backing track for long, meditative journeying. That spring we had to make do with an inferior singer some way off; but, sadder still, that first bird never returned the following year, so I never had the privilege of hearing his song again.

Birds don't live very long, and nightingale depletion in the UK means that so many birds don't return the following year. Once they mate, they stop singing. The music becomes weaker and, one by one, their song starts later at night and ends a little earlier in the morning. Eventually a moment arrives when the nightingale knows it's time to stop, and there ends the season of song. The nights become quiet and the phenomenon finishes for another year. The birds' day-song will continue into the summer and throughout the hatching period, but the great spectacle of the night-song is over.

There is a curious timing to the song's end, just at the point in the spring when the verdant blushes of that season's explosion feel established. I can only liken it to when a child reaches puberty and a door is walked through, an innocence shed, a vulnerability lost, stability in the world reached. The nightingale lullabies that soothed the nurturing sleep of the land are no longer needed and the bird's watch over nature's bedroom is over.

The Emperor and the Nightingale

In years gone by, nightingales stretched all the way east into China. However, they were rare birds in those lands, so it was considered a fortunate event to hear one. And so it was that a nightingale came to live in the woods that overhung a great river in the country ruled over by a great and powerful Emperor. The Emperor lived in a palace that was known for its splendid craftsmanship and ornate beauty. It was built of porcelain and glistened in the light of the many candles and lanterns that illuminated the vast complex. His gardens were tended by a fleet of gardeners, who made sure that every flower was perfect and everything was in order. Despite this, the Emperor rarely walked in the gardens, for he was old and preferred to stay inside with his books and courtiers.

He prided himself on being surrounded by the most beautiful objects in the world and was showered with gifts from across his kingdom and from admirers in far-distant lands. One day the Emperor received a book that told of all the wonders of his kingdom. It described how stately the Emperor's lands were, how bountiful the harvests, the vineyards and the views, but that the pinnacle of his dominion was the nightingale that sang from a tree leaning out across the great river. So stunning was his song that travellers from far-distant lands came in boats just to hear him sing, and fishermen who could not afford the time to stop and rest couldn't resist slowing their vessels to float unhurriedly beneath this enchanting song. The Emperor demanded that his head courtier tell him more about the bird in the book. But the courtier had never come across the nightingale.

The Emperor demanded that this nightingale was brought to him that evening, or great punishments would be meted out. In a panic, the head courtier flew about the palace, asking every servant and maid, stable boy and page if they knew of this singing nightingale. No one in the palace dared answer, but of course all of them did. The head courtier happened upon a young kitchen girl, just eight years old, who told the courtier that she knew of this bird and could lead him to it. The girl took the courtier through the gardens, out beyond the Emperor's palace walls and into the forest, where they walked for what seemed like many miles. They passed all sorts of animals making noises along the way: a lowing cow, a pond frog and, once they reached the banks of the great river, the whinnies of the river dolphins. To all of these sounds the courtier exclaimed, 'That must be the nightingale,' for he knew nothing of the outside world and the songs it sang.

Finally, there in the tree reaching far over the river, was the nightingale, simply attired in a light grey-brown feather. The courtier seemed disappointed at how plain the bird looked, until the kitchen girl called up to him and asked if he would sing them his song. The nightingale, being an enthusiastic character, was happy to oblige and started his sweet song.

The courtier decided this bird would be a huge success in the palace and invited the bird back to the court to sing for the Emperor. The nightingale said that, although his song sounded far better in the woods, he would go to the palace nonetheless.

On their return to the palace, the whole court filled with the Emperor's admirers and dignitaries. The porcelain palace had been specially polished and glistened in splendour for this unique occasion. As the nightingale sang for the Emperor, tears welled in his eyes and rolled down his cheeks. Even more the bird sang and, as he did so, the Emperor's heart melted as it had never done in all his live-long years. So impressed was he by the song that he commanded that his own golden slippers were to be hung around the nightingale's neck, but the bird refused. 'I have been amply rewarded, good Emperor, by witnessing your tears. Nothing could surpass that honour.' And so he continued to sing.

It was duly decided that the nightingale was to stay in court and a silver cage was created for him. He was permitted two walks a day and one at night, escorted by twelve footmen, who all held the ribbon attached to the nightingale's leg so that he could not fly away. The whole town talked of nothing but the nightingale.

One day a large package arrived for the Emperor labelled just 'Nightingale'. It was a gift from the Emperor of Japan, and in it stood a nightingale, but not of the feathered kind. This bird was a mechanical automaton, a wind-up silver imitator bejewelled with huge sapphires, rubies and other gemstones so radiant that the bird sparkled as his wings quivered when he 'sang'. Around his neck was a note saying: 'The Japanese Emperor's nightingale is a poor imitation compared to that of the Emperor of China.' But people adored this new nightingale, and the Japanese messenger who brought the gift was instantly promoted to Imperial Nightingale Wrangler-in-Chief.

The Emperor invited the two birds to sing together. 'What a duet it will be,' all the courtiers exclaimed. And so the two birds tried, but it didn't sound pleasant. The real nightingale sang whatever song came into his head, but the imitator bird sang by rote. Despite singing the self-same song over and over again, he never tired and could sing all day and all night for the Emperor and the courtiers, who adored his jewelled coruscation. The Emperor called back the true nightingale to sing again, but the bird was nowhere to be seen. He had flown out of an open window back to his woods.

'The ungrateful wretch,' the courtiers cried. 'Luckily we still have the best bird.' And so the new nightingale sang the same beautiful song again, for the thirty-fourth time. The music master declared, 'For you see, ladies and gentlemen, with the real bird one never knows what to expect, but with this bird, everything sounds just as designed, nothing is left to chance.'

And so this nightingale was raised to the lofty position of Grand Imperial Singer-to-Sleep of the Emperor. Great public concerts were held and voluminous books were written about this bird. Soon the Emperor and all his men knew his song by heart, and everywhere you went you could hear bakers and blacksmiths, silversmiths and street urchins reciting his reliable song, 'Zizizizizi, jug, jug, jug, jug, jug!'

One night, as the bird sang by the Emperor's bedside, out of his 'beak' came a ping, twang, churk, whirrrrrr sound, and his song ground down to a silent halt. The Emperor called his physician, who was unable to help; so he called the watchmaker who, with his loops and lenses, looked deep into the nightingale's workings. The diagnosis was not good. The mechanical bird's cogs had been badly worn and to replace them would change his song immeasurably. Instead a small repair was made, and strict orders were given for our bird to sing only once a year, for he had suffered from too much exertion.

This came as a great sadness to the citizens of the land who had grown to adore hearing this mechanical nightingale's singing. The Emperor was also devastated. After five long years, his sadness grew to sickness and the much-loved ruler fell gravely ill, as though he was ready to fly away himself. Word spread of the Emperor's impending death and the palace was made silent, with mats and soft shoes worn, so as not to make any noise or disturbance. He lay on his bed, pale and stiff, hardly breathing.

The Emperor opened his eyes. There he saw Death sitting on his chest, wearing the Emperor's gown, handling his gold sword and holding his silk banners. All around the room peered the familiar faces of those the Emperor had known and lost during his lifetime. These were the faces of his deeds – good ones and bad. 'Do you not remember?' each face cried, one after the other. 'Do you not remember?' And they each recited parts of his life, which made cold sweat run down his forehead. 'No, I shall not remember!' he cried out. 'Bring music, music, music. Sound the drums of China, lest I hear your words.' But on went their whisperings, and Death nodded in acknowledgement to each of their reminders.

'Music,' the Emperor implored, louder still. 'Sing, my precious little golden bird. Have I not brought you gifts and hung my golden slippers about your neck. Sing, I beg you, sing!'

But the bird stood silent, and all the while Death stared through his hollow eyes at the Emperor, and the palace was blanketed in unearthly silence.

Just then, at the window, arrived the real nightingale, who had heard of the Emperor's illness. He had come to sing to him of comfort and hope. And as he burst into song, the phantom faces melted back into the shadows. Even Death listened, willing the nightingale to 'Sing on, little bird. Sing on.'

The nightingale replied, 'Only if you return that sword, give back the Emperor's gown, his banners and his crown.' And as Death yielded, the blood flowed more quickly through the Emperor's weakened body, and Death turned into a grey mist and poured out of the window into the night.

'Thank you, thank you,' the Emperor declared. 'Little heavenly bird, I have known you from old. I cursed you for leaving me, and now you return to save my life. How can I reward you for your gifts?'

'You have already,' replied the nightingale. 'When first I sang for you, it brought tears to your eyes and, for a singer, that is a greater gift than any precious gemstone. Now you must sleep to grow your strength. I will continue my song to aid your slumber.'

The next morning, as the sun reached the window, the Emperor awoke, restored. He found his palace empty, as all the servants and courtiers had thought him dead. But still the nightingale was singing. 'Stay with me always,' asked the Emperor, 'but sing to me only when you please. I shall break the other nightingale into a thousand pieces.'

'Please, no,' said the nightingale. 'He did his best – keep him near your side. I cannot build my nest here or live in your palace, so let me come and go as I please, and I will sing to you of all the things that make you thoughtful and make you happy. I will tell you about all those who are sorrowful and those who are gay. My songs will tell you of all the good and evil that you cannot see. This little songbird will fly far and wide to the fisherman's hut, the farmer's home and to many places along the way, far from your palace and your court. For, Emperor, I love your heart more than I will ever love your crown. I will sing for you all these tales, if you promise me one thing.'

'All that I have is yours,' cried the Emperor.

'You must promise me one thing only,' asked the nightingale, 'and that is to not tell a soul that you have a tiny bird companion. This way, all will go well – better even than before.' And with that, the bird flew away.

Within moments of the nightingale taking leave, and thinking the Emperor was dead, in came the servants to take care of his body. And there they stood, in shock as the Emperor simply smiled and said, 'Good morning.'

CHAPTER TEN

EMPERORS AND NIGHTINGALES

The nightingale has found his perch in fables and tales across the world, some of which stand alone, and others that connect to lyrics or a musical instrumental. In every story the bird metamorphoses from one person's or one culture's nightingale, with all their associations, into another. He proves to be a transgressive bird, flitting from character to quandary in the most light-footed way. When I look at the nightingale in verse and literature, I cannot but feel that the bird is rather cheated of his rightful existence, with all that dark mythologising and burdensome woe, determined by our own projections. The English naturalist, illustrator and botanist James Bolton wrote in 1794, 'Not only in the time of Pliny, but long before him, and since, down to this day, this poor bird has been the butt of whining lovers, theatrical writers, romancers, novelists, poets, poetasters, and liars of many other denominations.'[13]

To echo one of the warnings from 'The Owl and the Nightingale' (see page 187), the sheer quantity of literature, prose, poetry and music dedicated to, and featuring, our bird is so profuse that, if read out loud non-stop, it would probably take an entire nightingale season to achieve. To spare the ears of my dear readers, I have touched on just a few of the well-known (and also, I hope, some less common) contributions to the canon. One day the encyclopaedia of nightingale verse will be published in full, but for now consider this my 'singer's digest' – some choice scratchings in the inky quill-pen of a nightingale's feather.

Andersen's emperor

There is no story about the nightingale that captures both the fragility and sensitivity of the bird's song and our relationship with this avian

[13] James Bolton, *The Nightingale in the Poetry and Science of the Long Eighteen Century*, https://www.liverpool.ac.uk/literature-and-science/essays/nightingale/

icon as effectively as Hans Christian Andersen's *Nattergalen*, more commonly known as 'The Emperor and the Nightingale'. For many people, this story is their first introduction to the bird's haloed voice. The tale was first published in 1843 in Denmark, where Andersen lived, and brings together numerous strands of the many labels assigned to the nightingale.

For Andersen, the nightingale might have been a meditation on unrequited love. He fell in love with the great Swedish opera singer Jenny Lind, who declined his affections. Lind gained the moniker 'The Swedish Nightingale' due to her association with Andersen, who was well practised at unrequited love, which became a constant throughout his life.

It's possible that Andersen was inspired to craft his nightingale tale by John Keats's 'Ode to a Nightingale', which was written more than a decade earlier, in 1819. Keats wrote the famously sombre poem in his anguish following his brother's death from tuberculosis. Andersen's father had also died of tuberculosis, as too, eventually, did Keats in 1821 in Rome, a city that fascinated Andersen. While there is no record of Andersen having read or written about Keats's 'Ode', it does refer to the two main characters of Andersen's fable:

> Thou wast not born for death, immortal Bird!
> No hungry generations tread thee down.
> The Voice I hear this passing night was heard.
> In ancient days by emperor and clown.

In 'The Emperor and the Nightingale' we see the themes of reality and mechanical representation brought to the fore. Startlingly ahead of his time, Andersen may have been enthused by encounters with early forms of cinema. The inventions of music boxes such as the fantascope, the zoetrope and the stroboscope in the 1830s revealed rudimentary prototypes of the mechanical replication of the natural world. Twenty-five years ahead of the Edison phonograph, which later turned into the gramophone around the turn of the century, there was a boom in music boxes. When Andersen wrote 'The Emperor and the Nightingale' production of such items was in full swing, with 10 per cent of Switzerland's exports then comprising these toy devices (far more than watches, at the time).

In his story Andersen manages to conflate the technological revelations of the day with ancient foreign mysticism, tapping into powerful themes that are present in so many fairy tales: nature as the messenger, the guide and the healer. But it is the inverted 'Pied Piper' role of the nightingale, as the stranger invited into this community, that is so enduring and well cast in the use of our bird. Andersen maintains the nightingale's role as outsider throughout, but reveals his vulnerability once subjugated to this hermetic world, until eventually he is outcast for his capricious unwillingness to obey. Here is maybe one of the first elegies or proto-tales concerning the very modern concept of biomimicry. Andersen has captured so effectively and presciently humanity's constant endeavours to conquer and improve on nature, and yet nature's ability to reach the heart in a way that no device ever can. The tale feels more relevant today than ever before.

Aesop's nightingale

Childhood fascination with nightingales is not only due to Andersen. Alongside his 'fairy' tales, *Aesop's Fables* are a standard of traditional European childhood. Little is known about Aesop, and none of his writings survive; he probably lived in ancient Greece around 600 NQ Aesop was a story collector, a fabulist and teller; a former slave – probably from Africa – who supposedly became a wise elder. He created around fifty allegories using animal pairings, with each species acting as a caricature of human folly. 'The Hawk and the Nightingale' (or 'The Hawk, the Nightingale and the Birdcatcher') is mentioned in Hesiod's poem *Works and Days*, written about 700 NQ but Aesop adopted it in his role as collector of oral stories, renewing and updating it:

> 'And now I will tell a fable for princes who themselves understand.' Thus said the hawk to the nightingale with speckled neck, while he carried her high up among the clouds, gripped fast in his talons.

THE·HAWK AND·THE NIGHTINGALE

In earlier versions of this fable, the hawk initially advises the nightingale that there is no point struggling, that 'he is a fool who tries to withstand the stronger'. The story began as a fable about the triumph of power and might. In later adaptations it evolved, with the hawk offering clemency if the nightingale will sing his famous music. Alas, the bird is too scared to utter more than a shrill note, so he is eaten by the hawk (or a kite in Jean de La Fontaine's *Le Milan el le Rossignol*; or a cat in the Russian Ivan Krylov's 'The Cat and the Nightingale').

Original references to the Aesop version describe some bloodthirsty and heartbreaking descriptions, which are surprisingly un-child-friendly to our modern ears. These subtle changes in narrative over time disperse into separate renditions, often swapping sympathies from the nightingale to the hawk, according to the morals of the storyteller in question. La Fontaine's version warns a stark 'An empty stomach has no ear.'

'The Labourer and the Nightingale'

In this tale Aesop uses the nightingale in a very different way, shrewdly outwitting a clumsy labourer from eating him:

> A Labourer lay listening to a nightingale's song all through a long summer's night. So pleased was he with the song that the next night he laid a trap for the bird and captured it.
>
> 'Now that I have caught thee,' he cried, 'you shall always sing for me.'
>
> 'Us Nightingales never sing in cages,' said the bird.

'Then I'll eat thee,' replied the Labourer. 'I have often heard that a toasted nightingale is a dainty meal.'

'Pray, kill me not,' exclaimed the Nightingale. 'Let me free, and I'll teach you three things of far better worth than my poor little body.'

The Labourer let him free, and the Nightingale flew up to a branch of a tree and spoke quietly: 'Never believe a promise spoken by a captive; that's the first thing. Then again: Keep what you have. And my third piece of advice is: Sorrow not over what is lost for ever.'

Then the songbird flew away.

By the twenty-first century most of *Aesop's Fables* had softened, over 2,500 years of retelling and rewriting. However Aesop's 'The Hawk and the Nightingale' indicates the darker origins of the nightingale's place in our collective mythology ...

The ancients

Our bird is also said to be 'Homer's nightingale'. Homer's *Odyssey* is one of the earliest records of the ancient myth of Philomela and Tereus, a classic tale of lament. The Roman poet Ovid, who lived between 43 ᴺᴼ and ᴹᴿ 18, provides the first telling of the story in his *Metamorphoses*, and this is repeated and echoed through Shakespeare, Chaucer, John Gower and into T. S. Eliot's *The Waste Land*. Ovid's rendition goes as follows:

Tereus, King of Thrace and son of Ares, was married to Procne, who was the sister to Philomela. Procne asked her husband if she could visit Philomela or bring her sister home, to spend time together.

King Pandion of Athens, their father, was uncertain about letting his last remaining daughter out of his protection, but entrusted Tereus to take care of her, asking him to look after Philomela as if she were his own daughter. Tereus agreed, but on the journey back to Thrace his lust for his sister-in-law grew. On arrival, he took her to the woods, where in a small lodging he raped her and threatened her to keep silent. But Philomela, in her defiance, infuriated Tereus, who cut out her tongue and banished her to this lodging.

Unable to speak, Philomela wove her story into a tapestry and had it sent to her sister. Procne was so enraged by this news that she took her own son by Tereus and murdered him in retribution, cooking him into a meal with which to feed her husband. After the meal, she presented Tereus with the severed head of her son.

Enraged by this conspiracy, Tereus took sword in pursuit of the sisters. As he was about to catch them, they prayed to the gods to be turned into birds to escape his violence. The gods obliged, turning Procne into a swallow and Philomela into a nightingale. Tereus was

PHILOMEL ·AND· PROGNE.

later turned into a hoopoe, a bird whose crest represents his royal status and whose long, sharp beak suggests his violent nature.

What is it within the nightingale's song that inspired such a tale of inherent violence and loss, we might ask. From a powerful signifier of spring and life and hope, the nightingale has been accorded far more layered and grave symbolisms, which transfuse later attempts to capture the bird and his magic. Is it the unnatural challenge of the nightingale's musical message? Perhaps it was our obsession with those 'first gods', and their import for our subsequent less moral world, that allowed the tragic and woeful 'Philomela' to endure in song and poetry down the millennia. Thank goodness we see writers, poets and dramatists draw out the affirmative associations of love and joy later on, as if to release our bird from these adverse allegations; however, the juxtaposition of the themes of joy and sorrow remains.

English fame

Despite the numerous times that nightingales appear in stories and folk songs, there is surprisingly little folklore around the bird in the British Isles – 'folklore' here meaning the interpretation of the bird in locally held proverbs, instructional texts and customary practice, passed down anonymously through oral tradition. Nightingales are widely associated with love and loss and, alongside the cuckoo, are a marker for the spring, but they are largely absent in Britain from our traditional oral-led stories. Edward A. Armstrong, the author of *The Folklore of Birds*, believed that 'the bird would hardly deserve mention here were it not for its eminence in literary traditions. These illustrate certain aspects of evolution and transmission of beliefs about birds in England, such as the reluctance of country people to accept literary bird lore into folklore.'

It would seem that the association of nightingales with human failings remained absent from the lore of the land – at least so far as we can tell, from what evidence survives today.

One of the best-known nightingale tales comes from the collections of the Brothers Grimm and concerns a deal forged with the blindworm (sometimes called a slow-worm). It's a story that occurs again and again throughout mainland Europe, in various tellings. It seems that both the blind-worm and the nightingale were once thought to have only one eye each. The nightingale asked to 'borrow' the blindworm's eye, as he was invited to a wedding (sometimes to the wedding of a wren, a bird ubiquitous in folklore). The blind-worm obliged, or maybe the nightingale stole the eye and then refused to return it. As a consequence, our nightingale has to stay awake all night, for fear of the blind-worm returning to reclaim his lost eye.

The nightingale and blind-worm / glow-worm pairing appears across Finland and France, England and Germany, and is picked up in the 1832 poem 'The Nightingale and the Glow-Worm' by poet and hymn writer William Cowper. This version ends with a somewhat more light-hearted outcome:

The Nightingale and the Glow-Worm

> A nightingale, that all day long
> Had cheered the village with his song,
> Nor yet at eve his note suspended,
> Nor yet when eventide was ended,
> Began to feel, as well he might,
> The keen demands of appetite;
> When, looking eagerly around,

He spied far off, upon the ground,
A something shining in the dark,
And knew the glow-worm by his spark;
So, stooping down from hawthorn top,
He thought to put him in his crop;
The worm, aware of his intent,
Harangued him thus right eloquent:
'Did you admire my lamp,' quoth he,
'As much as I your minstrelsy,
You would abhor to do me wrong,
As much as I to spoil your song,
For 'twas the self-same power divine
Taught you to sing, and me to shine,
That you with music, I with light,
Might beautify and cheer the night.'
The songster heard his short oration,
And warbling out his approbation,
Released him, as my story tells,
And found a supper somewhere else.

Here the clever glow-worm outwits the bird. In this – perhaps naive – iteration, God's creatures are all equal and never invoke harm upon one another. This light-hearted ditty seems in such contrast to the violence exhibited in the story of Philomela. But I want to redeem the nightingale's playful association by ending this collection of the bird's folk appearances with a translation that I have a long-time affection for and never tire of reading. 'The Donkey and the Nightingale' is taken from fables by Ivan Krylov. This encounter between the two creatures captures an absurd, yet superbly barbed commentary on taste and elegance.

The nightingale and the rose

In the great British poetry of the nightingale, the bird acts as a canvas on which many shades of emotion and interpretation have been painted – so many different roles have nightingales played throughout the ages: 'the single most important motif in all world poetry', according to the author and naturalist Mark Cocker.

The nightingale's first reference in England appeared in *Aenigmata* by Aldhelm, a seventh-century Anglo-Saxon poet and scholar. He recognised a nightingale's return in spring as symbolising Christ's resurrection. The bird goes on to appear in many forms throughout the centuries, ranging from a symbol of godly devotion to a noisy nuisance. Take this expression of frustration with his late-night filibustering from an anonymous *Greek Anthology*:

> Leaf-loving nightingales, loquacious sex,
> Sleep quietly, I beg, and cease your din.

The poetic canon of the nightingale cannot be discussed without looking first to Persian mystical poetry's reverence for the nightingale and the rose. The nightingale serves as metaphor for different forms of love – the nightingale as the poet or devoted/forlorn lover. His yearning for the perfect, cold, thorny and proud rose is often also seen as the longing for spiritual devotion and God.

'The Conference of the Birds' (*Mantiq-ut-Tayr*), a masterpiece of twelfth-century Persian poetry written by the Sufi poet Farid ud-Din Attar, exemplifies this relationship. In this story the birds of the world come together to decide that they need a head, or sovereign. The crowned hoopoe bird tells them they must embark on a long, perilous journey to find their great leader – the Simorgh, a large mythical bird with great powers. Each bird represents a human fault or failing that holds us back from full enlightenment, and of course the journey teaches them great lessons. When the birds reach the end of their quest, they look for the Simorgh in the lake and see their own reflection: the great leader of the birds is their collective self. As the journey unfolds, the nightingale – the 'amorous nightingale' and the 'nightingale of the Garden of Love' – claims not to be able to endure the expedition and declares he is satisfied by love of the rose. He is warned against being distracted from seeking self-improvement by the 'passing' love that 'has many thorns'.

The nightingale and the rose appear together once again in classical poetry. Take Thomas Lodge's *Scilla's Metamorphosis* of 1589:

> A Nightingal gan sing; but woe the lucke;
> The branch so neare her breast, while she did quike her
> To tune her head, on sodaine gan to pricke her.

Here, as in many other poems, the bird keeps herself (often the female in classical British poetry, as inherited from traditional assumption) awake by pressing her breast against the thorn. This theme is absent from any folklore in both Britain and France, but Oscar Wilde's heartbreaking short story 'The Nightingale and the Rose' is a meditation on the brutal nature of love and borrows heavily from the Persian tradition. Pressing his breast against the thorn to 'turn the white rose red' with his life-blood, the bird offers his life to support a student in asking for the hand in dance of his tutor's daughter (who then turns down the student, on being offered jewels by another young man). Wilde is musing here on the artist's plight as he sacrifices his very soul, only for such fragile gifts to be dashed and cast aside for shiny, tasteless glitter.

Medieval poetry

'The Owl and the Nightingale' is a famed early example of Middle English debate poetry – a style of poetry shared with the French, in which opposing viewpoints were represented, often using the forms of animals or birds – known as bestiaries. The poem originates from the twelfth or thirteenth century, and is as fresh and entertaining a discourse as if it had been written today. It takes the form of a slanderous argument between the two eponymous birds as they critique each other's appearance, habits and musical prowess, from the nightingale's misguided choice of season and over-singing, to the owl's gloominess of song and association with the dark habits of the night.

The writer is unknown, but the colloquialisms suggest that it stems from Kent, Sussex or somewhere nearby – so prime nightingale territory. And it certainly makes me think that the writer had experienced the reality of nightingale song. As the owl states:

> 'But you sing all through the night,
> From evening til it's daylight,
> And carry on with your one song
> As long as ever the night goes on.
> Your wretched throat just croaks away,
> And doesn't stop by night or day.
> With a raucous din your pipings fill
> The ears of people wherever you dwell,
> And you give your song to so many
> That no one counts it worth a penny.
> Every pleasure may last so long
> That in the end it stops being fun.'

The owl's witty accusation of the nightingale song being overused and lacking in rectitude and reserve is wonderfully on-point. The gluttony of song that we experience from the nightingale each spring feels almost wasteful, when we have to wait ten and a half months for the next feast. While I would never get bored of hearing him, I have to know when to step away. The incessantness of the song throughout the night defies our human sense of economy, our interpretation of the 'proper' use of talent and skill. Yet such is the nature of the appetite of our ears that there really is only so much nightingale song you can handle per night. Once you have read the owl's quips and jests, you can never quite hear the nightingale in the same way again.

The nightingale was always going to feature heavily when wandering bards, troubadours and minstrels invoked the animal kingdom in their lyric poetry, for great entertainment. There's also Chaucer's 'The Cuckoo and the Nightingale', and then 'The Thrush and the Nightingale', 'The Clerk and the Nightingale' …

Lovers in the woods

For the Romantics, who endeavoured to contemplate nature in all its guises, the nightingale was similarly a bird that could not be ignored. Percy Bysshe Shelley said: 'A poet is a nightingale who sits in darkness, and sings to cheer its own solitude with sweet sounds; his auditors are as men entranced by the melody of an unseen musician, who feel that they are moved and softened, yet know not whence or why.' Few writers get as close as Shelley when placing their own artistic purpose upon our bird, as in this quote.

Now so much of our conversation around the survival of the nightingale echoes our concerns about the survival of our natural world.

Nightingales are deeply associated with our native brush, our woodlands, our 'pastoral' vision.

Milton, of course, has a lot to answer for, as the father of romantic nightingale poetry. His Sonnet 1, 'O Nightingale', depicts the battle between love and hate, in the guise of the nightingale and the cuckoo:

> O Nightingale, that on yon bloomy Spray
> Warbl'st at eeve when all the Woods are still,
> Thou with fresh hope the Lovers heart does fill,
> While the jolly hours lead on propitious May,
> Thy liquid notes that close the eye of Day,
> First heard before the shallow Cuccoo's bill
> Portend success in love; O if Jove's will
> Have linkt that amorous power to thy soft lay,
> Now timely sing, ere the rude Bird of Hate
> Foretell my hopeles doom in som Grove ny:
> As thou from yeer to yeer has sung too late
> For my relief; yet hadst no reason why,
> Whether the Muse, or Love call thee his mate,
> Both them I serve, and of their train am I.

There is a refreshing absence of lament and sorrow attached to the bird here – a reprieve from the many dour associations to come from the Romantics. Here, the nightingale represents a rather simple and traditional sense of love and hope, and success in love. The poor cuckoo (appearing again with the nightingale) is the bird of hate and the negative emotions of love, such as jealousy. The poet asks the nightingale to sing his 'liquid notes' for him before the cuckoo's 'rude' song, and speaks of the amorous power of the nightingale's 'soft lay' ('lay' here meaning a short lyric or song).

Samuel Taylor Coleridge, thankfully, took up this mantle to protect the nightingale from drowning in doom. His 'The Nightingale: A Conversation Poem' (1798) corrects Milton's 'Most musical, most melancholy' tag (from his *Il Penseroso*) and roots the bird in its nature:

> 'Most musical, most melancholy' bird!
> A melancholy bird! Oh! Idle thought!
> In nature there is nothing melancholy' ...
> 'Tis the merry nightingale
> That crowds, and hurries, and precipitates
> With fast thick warble his delicious notes,
> As he were fearful that an April night
> Would be too short for him to utter forth
> His love-chant, and disburthen his full soul
> Of all its music!

Coleridge instead attributes sorrow to lovelorn men wandering the night, and describes the nightingale as 'merry'. With its Gothic themes and rather abstract connections, his poem received a somewhat critical response from his contemporaries. But to me, his poem speaks honestly of the plenitude and compulsion of the nightingale's song. Coleridge seems to hear the bird in its place in nature, instead of the Philomel, burdened with its weight of grief.

The 'immortal bird'

Keats's 'Ode to a Nightingale' was his magnum opus. It was written somewhere in Hampstead just 200 years ago. Keats heard nightingales in his garden that year (it was an unusually early spring, by all accounts), and his close friend Charles Armitage Brown explained:

> In the spring of 1819 a nightingale had built her nest near my house. Keats felt a tranquil and continual joy in her song; and one morning he took his chair from the breakfast-table to the grass-plot under a plum-tree, where he sat for two or three hours. When he came into the house, I perceived he had some scraps of paper in his hand, and these he was quietly thrusting behind the books. On inquiry, I found those scraps, four or five in number, contained his poetic feelings on the song of the nightingale.

Keats's 'immortal bird' plays with the concepts of death and life, and dreams and reality. There is plenty of nature within the poem, but I can't help feeling that the truth of the nightingale is overlooked in favour of Keats's projections. A famously poetic reply to him, written much later by D. H. Lawrence while holidaying in Tuscany, says as much about us as it does about the nightingale:

> The viewless wings of Poesy carry him only into the bushes, not into the nightingale world. He is still outside…
>
> How astonished the nightingale would be if he could be made to realise what sort of answer the poet was answering to his song. He would fall off the bough with amazement…
>
> Hello! Hello! Hello! It is the brightest sound in the world: a nightingale piping up. Every time you hear it, you feel wonder and, it must be said, a thrill, because the sound is so bright, so glittering, it has so much power behind it.
>
> 'There goes the nightingale!' you say to yourself. It sounds in the half-dawn as if the stars were darting up from the little thicket and leaping away

into the vast vagueness of the sky, to be hidden and gone. But the song ringson after sunrise, and each time you listen again, startled, you wonder: 'Now *why* do they say he is a sad bird?'.

He is the noisiest, most inconsiderate, most obstreperous and jaunty bird in the whole kingdom of birds. How John Keats managed to begin his *Ode to a Nightingale* with 'My heart aches and a drowsy numbness pains my sense—' is a mystery to anyone acquainted with the actual song. You hear the nightingale silverily shouting 'What? What? What John?—Hearts aches and a drowsy numbness pains?—tra-la-la!-tri-li-lilylily.'[14]

Nature's poet

When it comes to accurate observation and a true knowing of the nightingale, for me none come as close as John Clare. Clare was known as the 'Labourer Poet' or the 'Northamptonshire peasant poet', and his work was largely disregarded until the twentieth century. His connection with nature, devoid of sentimentality or device, is palpable in his poetry. He was less educated than his contemporaries, being raised in relative poverty and subsidising his writing with work as a farm labourer and gardener. Clare grew up with oral traditions around him and invoked the colloquial language of his area to great effect in his work. 'The Nightingale's Nest' is a punctilious and tender observation of the nightingale's world:

> Creeping on hands and knees through matted thorn
> To find her nest, and see her feed her young.

This is Clare's journey into the nightingale's domain, so contrary to previous poetic works that centred the human condition within the nightingale.

---

[14] D. H. Lawrence, *D. H. Lawrence and Italy: Sketcher from Etoseen Places, Sea and Serdinia, Twilight in Italy* in *D. H. Lawrence Selected Library Criticism*, Heineman, 1955

Clare seems desperate to share the inner life of the bird, to bring others to find the nightingale as autonomous, and yet the poem's wonderful descriptions of her 'curious house' and her choice of undisturbed haunts also speak to our desecration of the landscape and natural world:

> See there! she's sitting on the old oak bough,
> Mute in her fears; our presence doth retard
> Her joys, and doubt turns every rapture chill.
> Sing on, sweet bird! may no worse hap befall
> Thy visions, than the fear that now deceives.

Clare wrote about the bird just sixteen years after Keats's 'Ode'. Clare said, of Keats and his nightingale: 'nature as she appeared to his fancies and not as he would have described here had he witnessed the things he described'. Ouch!

Clare's 'The Nightingale', written in 1832, is a wondrous transliteration of the bird's song into onomatopoeic prose. But this poem is more than impersonation, for it details a uniquely English embodiment of the bird. The madness that befell Clare in his later years is almost suggested here, as he internalises the spirit and tongue of our nightingale. He tried to capture the essence of the bird, while all around him the land was being enclosed and torn away from him and his fellow working men and women.

Since Aristophanes's 'tawney-throated partner' we have been trying to capture the nightingale's song in words, just as musicians have tried to capture what T. S. Eliot described as an 'inviolable voice' in *The Waste Land*. Poets have attempted to render, repurpose and lyrically ring the nightingale. For me, Clare came closest, but none have reduced his song so simply better than the Greek essayist Plutarch around ᴀᴅ 45. He wrote of a man who captured a nightingale for his dinner table and plucked it, but on finding so little to eat exclaimed: 'You are just a voice and nothing more.'

CHAPTER ELEVEN

GOODNIGHT, NIGHTINGALE:
STANDING UP FOR OUR BIRDS

The crow that's black, my little turtle dove,
Shall change its colour white
If I prove false to the songbird that I love.
The noonday shall sound as night, my love,
The noonday shall sound as night.

The hills shall fly, my little turtle dove,
The roaring billows burn
Before my heart shall suffer me to fail
Or I a traitor turn, my love,
Or I a traitor turn.

'Turtle Dove', traditional English folk song

The irony of nature conservation work is that, primarily, it doesn't involve working *with* nature, but working to limit the damage that humans are doing *to* nature. Left to her own devices, the natural world would be absolutely fine. But our help *is* needed and there is so much we can do. The nature-protection movement needs as many voices, hands and heroes as possible, working at all levels. But it is your time, your presence and, most importantly, your imagination that are most valuable.

First and foremost, become informed on the issues that surround and concern you – be that globally or locally. I am a great believer in starting local, with wherever your immediate community is working to protect or restore threatened wildlife-rich spaces. The Friends of the Earth local group networks bravely tackle issues that might be close to your heart, as well as those of which you may not have been aware. These include the protection of bees, air pollution, fossil-fuel divestment, tree cover, fracking, plastic in the ocean and rivers, and so many more issues. The Extinction Rebellion regional networks also provision local communities with well-informed and scientifically sound research and are hubs for action-based gatherings. Despite XR's reputation, you don't have to take direct action or get arrested in order to get involved. There's a place for writers, artists, strategists, therapists, marketeers, young and old – even those whose passion is spreadsheets.

How does all this help the nightingale? As the Scottish-American ecologist John Muir, one of the founding fathers of environmental protection, famously wrote of the environment in his book *My First Summer in the Sierra*: 'When we try to pick out anything by itself we find it hitched to everything else in the universe.' Such is the case of the nightingale that these birds can be identified as 'canaries in the mine'. In their precarious and vulnerable relationship with our land, they tell us the strength of the threads within the cord within the rope that ties us to Mother Nature. Nightingales, along with the environment they depend on, need your help, and there are so many ways you can do this.

Protect, restore and fund

On a local and global level, the current mantra on how to invite simple, achievable changes and gestures into our lives is: Protect, Restore and Fund. These are the headline terms in the journey of becoming more environmentally conscientious, and are what we must do – both individually, and collectively as a species – to combat the climate and ecological emergency. **Protect** the ecosystems that we have, and defend ecosystems under threat from development. **Restore** land, where possible, back to the best carbon-sequestering state, primarily through tree planting. And **fund** positive environmental and societal change, spending your money mindfully.

The erosion of our natural habitats is happening incrementally, but visibly, almost everywhere you look. The 2019 *State of Nature* report findings bear repetition here: a 13 per cent decline in average abundance of all terrestrial and fresh-water species (with the most emphatic decline in the last decade); and the UK will not meet most of the global 2020 targets that it committed to, through the Convention on Biological Diversity. We are seeing the destruction of 108 ancient woodlands for HS2's build across England. Local councils, without consultation, are removing city trees – as has already happened, yet luckily was mostly thwarted by the coordinated actions of residents, in Sheffield. We are experiencing the unbelievable abuse and neglect of our river systems, with dry river beds caused by unregulated water extraction, and water poisoning from agricultural run-off, unopposed industrial waste and untreated sewage being dumped illegally – all uncontested. We live in a time when the greatest threat comes from apathy, so remember: every level of involvement counts.

I am particularly impressed with projects that invite participation from communities and volunteers. They pioneer the combination of action-based participatory work populated by hearty folk who know how to hold sociable and fun-filled experiences. Conservation, although tough work, should be fun. One example is Feedback, a national campaign group working to regenerate nature by transforming our food system – food production being the single biggest impact that humans have on the environment. Focusing on the issues around food waste, they combine hard-hitting investigative research, mass public 'feasts' and on-the-ground pilot projects to encourage a better food

NIGHTINGALE'S NEST.

system. Its 'Gleaning Network' is a fabulous project, inviting volunteers to combat food waste by heading out into the fields after harvest to gather unwanted crops left to rot. And the Ecosystem Restoration Camps enterprise is an international movement establishing dozens of camps that welcome and train volunteers to get active in reviving land degraded through soil erosion, drought and deforestation. It restores the land and the soil with permacultural practices, moving previously barren landscapes back into vibrant food-producing gardens and wildlife havens.

I am also a great believer in the impact of the guerrilla tactics used by environmental campaigners to do clean-up work, independent of any official body and without permission of landowners. A dear friend and environmental barrister, Paul Powlesland, has pioneered many local actions in and around London, particularly centred on the River

Roding, which he is helping to restore. One of the ways he is doing this is through 'Positive Trace Parties'. These informal affairs involve small groups of friends descending on areas of what we would consider wasteland, combining a day-long social with rubbish removal, tree-planting and general habitat improvement. At one such event fifty people gathered; music was played, food was cooked and a party atmosphere was created that resulted in a stretch of the plastic-choked River Roding being left free of the signs of human neglect and a much healthier place for wildlife. In Paul's words, 'If we wait for the leaders or local authorities to sort things out, they never will. We can't wait for their permission, we have to take matters into our own hands.'

This approach challenges us to rethink the way we view our unused land and forgotten places as dirty, contaminated, soiled and unimportant. It can be difficult to do away with vanity when considering where to lend our support, but we need to remove our bias when offering it. This is the nature lover's version of a street-dog rescue. Aren't these marginal places just as worthy of our care and attention as a national park, particularly if their undisturbed inaccessibility makes them better species havens than well-trodden beauty spots?

Every gesture counts, even if you just bring a bag with you on walks, to collect litter. Why not take on the positive-trace idea yourself. There are so many ways that you alone, or with friends, can select places that need some love and attention and take on that same mantle of guerrilla conservation – gardening, tree-planting and litter-picking, with some playfulness thrown in for good measure. As Feedback's founder, Tristram Stuart, says, 'To beat the opposition you have to throw a better party.'

Nightingales don't tend to visit gardens, but follow the advice of the RSPB's Adrian Thomas, in maintaining whatever green area you have as wildlife-friendly. We need to do away with the old-fashioned appeal of order and neatness, as epitomised in the closely cropped British lawn. The maintenance of messy spaces that are allowed to run wild encourages a boom in invertebrates, molluscs and naturally occurring weeds, which in turn support so many more birds, small mammals, hedgehogs and amphibians than a manicured garden environment.

If you own or rent land in areas of the UK where nightingales breed, it is well worth exploring how you can make it more nightingale-friendly, and perhaps even encourage the re-establishment of your own resident population. The BTO has published a superb pamphlet called 'Managing Scrub for Nightingales', which is easily downloadable for free on their website, and which talks through all the ways you can encourage and develop the right habitat. These are also havens for other songbirds, so they are worthwhile even if your chances of becoming a nightingale nursery are slim.

Your environmental actions start at home: get vocal about what you see and don't agree with. Write to your MPs and local councillors, and lobby for more resourcing of our natural spaces. Get online and use social media to share information, events, petitions and projects that need greater awareness. Campaigning leaders like Chris Packham, Caroline Lucas and George Monbiot are excellent at disseminating hard-hitting facts, as well as positive stories of success and forward movement. Help their algorithms by following, liking and reposting. Put posters up in your windows and nail your colours to the mast. Tut-tutting at the issues achieves absolutely nothing. Remember: only get angry if you get active.

Funding positive and environmentally friendly enterprises is one area in which we can really start to make a difference. It is one of the most directly impactful ways we can ensure that our daily lives are not supporting the destruction and exploitation of the world's natural resources. Follow where your money goes in the products and ingredients being used to make your food – its progeny, its environmental footprint and, of course, its packaging. There are wonderful UK-wide programmes for locally sourced and seasonal food, such as Growing Communities, which works to reform the food system via the national Better Food Traders network, who connect up similar schemes across the UK. Buying local and organic produce through similar schemes, or your local shops, as much as possible means that the carbon footprint of your purchase isn't costing the earth, and leaves a positive impact in the place where it is grown.

Examine all aspects of where your money lives – who it passes through, where it is invested – and make sure, wherever possible, that it can be directed into organisations that are working for sustainability in their sector. Where is your money banked and invested? Is getting the best return on your savings and pension plans worth it, knowing that your money might be invested in a fossil-fuel or mineral-extraction multinational? Where is your electricity sourced from? By paying a fraction more, could you be giving your money to a renewables-only provider? When buying clothes, could you choose second-hand, Fairtrade or organic garments over standard new fashion, remembering that one kilo of cotton (equivalent to one shirt and a pair of trousers) requires 20,000 litres of water to grow and manufacture it? How much meat is in your diet? Did you know that to produce one kilo of beef creates about 13.3 kilos of carbon dioxide? This is the same quantity of CO_2 as is released from burning about 6 litres of petrol! Reducing your meat intake essentially lowers your carbon emissions.

Lastly, donate to causes that you believe in – be they local projects (which often make a bigger difference) or larger NGOs that work on campaigns at national and international levels.

Will the next generation hear the nightingale?

The potential absence of this bird and his song from our land is an unthinkable idea. Imagine it to be like the British Library losing a wing; a radio station being taken off air; the Beatles', Tchaikovsky's and Billie Holiday's recorded catalogues being removed from the world. If we lose the nightingale, we would only be able to describe to our children what it was like to hear his music. And it is the children who most need it. Getting nature under their fingernails, up their noses and into their imaginations is one of the most important educational experiences a child can have, outside the family. It is the classroom for raising wise, centred and grounded humans.

I'm firmly of the belief that a dirty childhood is a healthy childhood. If you have children of your own, brokering that opportunity for them to spend as much time as possible outdoors, unrestricted and untethered, is, I believe, a child's necessity and right. Create opportunities for your child and others to have the freedom to explore outdoors and, where possible, without the constant watchful eye of an adult. Being allowed to explore, take risks, investigate, be inquisitive of the land and develop a familiarity with the natural environment will pay off handsomely later in their lives. In whatever way you can invite this into the lives of children you know, I unreservedly encourage it. I remember nature being my best friend and closest companion while growing up, and the skills and sensitivities I learned from my time outdoors have supported and inspired me throughout my life.

Nature taught me resourcefulness, resilience, tenderness and accountability for my actions; it enabled me to be comfortable with solitude and quietness, stimulated my ingenuity and patience, and resolved my deep-seated fear of the dark. The experience of going in search of nightingales offers the wonderful possibility to bridge a child's imagination, through the birds' prominence in story and song, into reality. The animation of those stories, by hearing and perhaps even seeing a nightingale, can breathe this natural theatre alive for a child. Save the £250 cost of a family trip to a West End production of your child's favourite novel and instead go on a nightingale trip, having read a Hans Christian Andersen or Oscar Wilde nightingale tale. It's free, and you can leave as soon as your kids get tired and tetchy.

Aside from my touring and recording as a musician, I am also artistic director of a music organisation that I founded fifteen years ago called the Nest Collective. It's grown into an organisation that creates live events, acoustic festivals, campfire concerts, nature-connection projects, pilgrimages, song-collecting trips and ceilidhs, bringing music

into communities and outdoor spaces. Our events aim to connect people with nature, often involving fire at their heart. The most prolific of these projects are the 'Singing with Nightingales' annual events, but I am constantly looking for innovative and creative ways to give people permission to get out into green spaces and, through musical experiences, deepen their confidence to spend more time outside. All these projects have been inspired by a lifetime of self-initiated outdoor gatherings, usually with music.

I had the good fortune of being empowered to make these unique gatherings through an upbringing over the summertime within, and staffing on, the children's charity Forest School Camps. FSC taught us the fundamentals in creating a home and a community out in the woods, with not much more than a box of matches and our voices. I was initiated into this (sadly) rare relationship with the outdoors from a young age, and it gave me a unique gift in the confidence to co-create ways to experience the natural world, in playful and meaningful participation with other children and adults. The journey to protecting our natural heritage begins with brokering deeper relationships like this between the land and the communities that live upon her. But entwined with that necessity is the right for each of us to self-determine, with constant respect for the land, how those endeavours might manifest themselves. How do we create a national sense of sovereignty and allow ourselves to forge our own stories, as we get to know our natural world better?

My six weeks each year of taking intimate groups out into the dark woods for 'Singing with Nightingales' events have introduced me to many different personal relationships with the outdoors. It has also allowed me many nights to wonder what different expressions this country might employ to create a more enchanted existence with nature. The possibilities are endless, and the passion projects I have experienced, run by fellow nature lovers, are inspiring. The UK is experiencing a blossoming of new circles and communities working to heal our broken relationship with the land, strengthen our connection and deepen our knowledge. These wilderness camps, music camps, rewilding centres, forest schools, field-study centres and more are all out there and make for memorable experiences.

Nightingale success stories

Lodge Hill on the Hoo Peninsula in Kent is a curious example of the benefit of neglect. It was owned by the Ministry of Defence from Victorian times until 1961 and hosts one of the UK's largest populations of nightingales. It was an 'ordnance depot', storing explosives in bunkers, so it was heavily fenced, abandoned and left to develop naturally. It has since been designated a Site of Special Scientific Interest (SSSI), due to the profound biodiversity within its 'ancient woodland and unimproved grassland'. The RSPB called it the 'UK's most important home for nightingales', and the 2012 BTO Nightingale Survey counted eighty-five singing males on the land, accounting for more than 1 per cent of the total UK population. But such attractive 'wasteland' caught the eye of Homes England, who bought the site, and talk of developing the area for housing began. A wonderful response from the public, coordinated by local and national wildlife groups, fought for two decades to fend off the plan. In 2018 the first major victory concerning the development saw the 2,000 planned homes reduced to 500 and removed to just outside the SSSI land, although it is feared this will still impact upon the special area and its nightingale population.

Nightingales at Knepp

Knepp Reminding Estate is a reimagining of the English farm turned into a prosperous West Sussex Serengeti. Husband and wife eco-visionaries, Charlie Burrell and Isabella Tree, have pioneered the UK's most famous nature-based solution to the habitat and biodiversity issues occurring worldwide, through their much-lauded rewilding project. Charles inherited this 3,500-acre (1,417-hectare) farm from his grandparents and spent seventeen years attempting to turn it into a profitable dairy and arable farm. By the year 2000 he had concluded that it wasn't possible on their heavy clay soils. They sold off the dairy herds and farm equipment to pay the farm's large debts and embarked on a project of 'process-led' nature restoration. With the help of Natural England, they began to employ the ideas of the Dutch ecologist Frans Vera on how the landscape could be self-directed to create a 'Biodiverse Wilderness Area in the Low Weald of Sussex'.

Their 'rewilding' concept is an experiment that has produced unmatched results in a rapid timespan – a model for allowing nature to dictate its own ability and restore its own fertility and abundance. It's a wonderful example of allowing nature's own balancing system to dictate events. The collaboration of species – including those grazing and browsing animals that are proxies of the herbivores that would have shaped our landscape in the past – and the particular land and soil needs have prevailed, despite the history of ploughing, chemical fertilisers and pesticides, over-extraction and weakened topsoil. Knepp basically relinquished control and handed nature the script to do whatever it wanted. In return, there is a proliferation of species such as nightingales, lesser-spotted woodpeckers and cuckoos, bats and dormice and a range of butterflies, which suddenly bring the place to life.

This haven they have created is a place where we can really start to observe and understand the behaviour of species in a way we've not been able to before. Knepp's team of biologists and conservationists closely monitors the progress, to provide detailed and inspiring inventories of how the land has responded.

The greatest success, for many people, of this sympathetic form of land stewardship is to see the turnaround of our most threatened native bird, the turtle dove, and how it has made a startling return at Knepp. There were 125,000 pairs of turtle doves in the UK in the 1960s and there are fewer than 5,000 today. Isabella Tree's best-selling book *Wilding* tells the story of the guesswork in understanding why these birds have thrived at Knepp. It is possibly due to the return of certain plants, such as vetch, fumitory and fluellin, which have tiny protein-rich seeds that the birds feed on, and which thrive in areas rootled by the pigs; as well as the nutrient-rich new shoots and sprouting and germination of seeds.

At Knepp a proliferation of nightingales has occurred that sing intensely all night long, and in competition with other successfully returned males. I will never forget a starry night there one May when the cuckoo also decided to sing all night alongside the nightingales, in an interspecies concert that you could only experience in a site with as much abundance as Knepp. Little sleep was had that night.

Nightingales aren't new to Knepp. Nine territories were identified on the estate in 1999, but by 2001 none were found. Two decades of rewilding later, Knepp is hosting nightingale walks. There were thirty-four territories in 2012, and of those, it was shown that the pairing/mating rates were distinctly higher than in other local areas and even on the continent. These birds were strong and successful specimens. The increase is a wonderful indicator; the land is in good shape and, through the nightingales, it shows. What is even more interesting, and needs more exploration, is the way the dynamic, shifting thorny scrub that the nightingales live in is one of the most biodiverse habitats there is, and it's where Knepp is finding most of its rarest birds, as well as an unprecedented abundance of biomass that is shifting the baseline for nature conservation. This scrub is a far more natural landscape for nightingales, and closely matches their European neighbours' habitat. They are happily settling within these 'growing out' hedgerows with cathedral-like hollow interiors, where the young nightingales can safely forage for insects in the leaf litter.

A vision of a 'one day' way

I have long dreamed there to be one utterly fanciful and romantic way that this call to bond further with nature and the nightingales – and all their legacy of appreciation – might take hold among friendship groups and families.

I like to imagine that, one day in a not-too-distant future, a ritual will exist annually every spring. England, having as many nightingales as it did before the 1960s (that is, in the hundreds of thousands), experiences, come early May, an exodus of people from their homes to go and '*do*' a 'Nightingaler'. Families and friends, couples and singletons, grandparents and grandchildren, community groups, work colleagues – whoever it pleases – will gather on gentle, dry nights with flasks of hot tea, snacks (maybe even a bottle of port or whisky), blankets and, at around 9 p.m., will leave their homes or the pub, or drive many hundreds of miles even, to head out to a nightingale hotspot. On the journey there, stories will be told of when each person first heard his song, and how wonderful it will be to hear this bird again after a long, cold winter; how much the spring has come on this year, how early or late it was, and other such seasonal reminiscences and observations.

When the destination is reached, a silence will fall upon the group, like when the lights go down at a concert, and a hush will reign. Intrepid steps are made into the brush to get close to a bird as quietly as possible and, when he is reached, blankets are spread and everyone cosies up to one another to start listening. I imagine this scene like an English equivalent of a Burns Night, but informally arranged on the leafy floor, amongst the hyacinthine scent of bluebells. There are kids curled up on parents' laps, friends resting their heads on each other's bellies or leaning back-to-back. After a while of just listening to the nightingale sing, out of someone's pocket comes an old tattered notebook with scraps of paper; maybe it's been handed down from a late parent, or gifted from a godmother when they were young. A phone light is discreetly turned on and, in hushed reverential voices, poems and songs and rounds and prose are recited or sung up towards our nightingale. Every offering is an heirloom received, found or chosen along life's way, savoured as being perfect for this annual moment. The opportunity to share something is passed around for anyone who wants to give a sonnet or a recitation. An improvised sharing evolves, unique to those present and to each year's mood. Some sharings are sombre and mournful, others are comical, with muted sniggers and irreverences. Some people are formal, others are casual; some are drunk, others are stoned; some are erotic, some are lonely, some are romantic, some are in remembrance, and some are in prayer. But all are in celebration of this bird, and of ourselves as sentient, sensitive beings, grateful for what might not have survived.

As the night ends and we drowsily make our way home, drunk on nightingale song and a bit woozy, I like to think the resounding feeling that everyone goes home with, exclaiming to one another, is not as I hear all the time today, 'Gosh, why don't we do this more often?', but more of a 'Wow – thank you, everyone. I am so pleased we do this every year.'

Call me a romantic (I've been called worse), but is this not the sort of restorative practice that could epitomise an idiosyncratic English escapade and be the most perfect way to gather for a night each spring?

Similar to the way European families go off on a day of foraging for fungi in autumn, this ritual – picking up from where May Day ceases to hold prominence, or even relevance, in our communities today – would be a baptism of each year's arrival of spring.

'We need *you* to paint the positive picture of how the world can be,' Caroline Lucas, MP, demands, and I agree. The nightingale's survival is in *our* hands. The crisis the nightingales, and our natural world, is experiencing is a failure of our imaginations to manifest what 'better' looks like. Finding our roles in the 'ecosystem' of nature protection is our ongoing challenge. I am of the firm belief that to change society's behaviours, we need to change people's minds, and to do that we have to go through their hearts. Art – be it music, theatre, fine art or any other vibrant way that we express our relationships to the world – is the most powerful agent in this campaign for ecological survival. We need every creative human bringing their voice to the chorus of climate action, and every member of the chorus becoming creative. Culture, it is said, eats strategy for breakfast. The policies of our political governance have so far failed. But if artists of all magnitudes and mediums agreed to utilise their profile to colonise as many of the mass media's platforms as they can, then the demands for change would become unavoidable, possibly even appealing. The power of this belief is being proved handsomely through two momentous campaigns: Music Declares Emergency and Culture Declares Emergency. Both these organisations are working to galvanise, empower and activate a unified voice within the music and arts sector, and the results are suggesting that change in those industries is coming fast. These look like hopeful signs.

I personally do my petitioning through gentle invitations to seek out and re-enchant the hidden, quiet, intangible and threatened. The 'Nightingaler', as described above, could be one such provocation – tender and unifying, a bespoke and poetic direct action in praise of this treasure on our own doorstep. This is just one way to find and play with the bit of nature that holds a spell that can light us up. The nightingale wields that power, but maybe for not much longer. You too can find your own nightingale or other bird, or tree or piece of ground, and way of celebrating them. For those who can and dare to, the reward is enormous. But, more crucially, you will some day become the one needed to tell these stories to those who didn't, and those to come who will never be able to.

The Moon Shines Bright (traditional English folk song)

> The moon shines bright
> And the stars give a light,
> In a little while it will be day.
> Rise, arise, awake thee, arise,
> And ever more watchful be.

NIGHTINGALE.

EPILOGUE

Oh grief, oh grief have I
For the songs they go to decay
The garden of England once bloomed her sound assault
Now destined for some bouquet
No roses in this display.

from 'The Garden Of England'
('Seeds of Love') by Sam Lee

The vocabulary we possess does not suffice to describe the conditions that we are confronting today. We now live in a frontier of climatic extremities and ecological tumult, which demands that we forge new language to articulate sentiments not yet witnessed by us, as modern humans. The cellist Anthony Albrecht, a 'Singing with Nightingales' guest and interpreter of Australian birdsong, merges classical improvisation and nature appreciation – an artistic practice that is in no way coincidental. Anthony is the son of Glenn Albrecht, the environmental philosopher who coined the word 'solastalgia' to describe the grief currently being felt for the loss of nature. The word is a neologism, blending *solace* and *nostalgia*; it denotes a sense of homesickness for a place that is no more; distress at the loss of a sense of place. We are losing not just our home, but also the home of our brother and sister species.

This term 'solastalgia' captures an ever-present sense that I have experienced many, many times in my work in the conservation of folk music. As a field recordist and collector of traditional songs for the last fifteen years, I have encountered solastalgia on a cultural level whenever I am out recording the fast-disappearing songs of the British Isles. Since I first headed out on recording trips to meet the elders of the English Gypsy and Irish and Scottish Traveller communities, I've recorded hundreds of people and families across England, Wales, Scotland and Ireland. In doing so, a much-ignored treasure trove of songs and stories has been preserved. But these song-carriers were, for me, the equivalent of the 'giant tuskers' – aged African elephants so old that their enormous ivories sweep the floor. These singers, like those wizened pachyderms, carry an ancient knowledge of their community and a lineage of songs going back centuries, and in some cases millennia. Every time I revisited a family, I'd find another of the singers had died – another person holding the last link to the music and stories of the past gone. This was a unique and beautiful forest, which on each visit was one tree fewer.

Another word that has been forged in response to the demise of ecological diversity is one created in 1996, which describes the final individuals of a species looking down the gun barrel of extinction.

'Endlings' is a term used for the last of a species that is going extinct, where there is just a handful left, which are effectively being nursed out of existence. The singers I was recording were, in their own way, 'endlings' – the last of their kind or the end of a line. Here was a people deprived of its way of life, suffering from endemic racism and societal indifference. The impact of this on Gypsy Travellers' health and mental well-being was shocking to witness. I'd grown to dearly love my time with these old folks and their families, as much for their rich, colourful characters as for the privilege of hearing their ancient songs sung in the way they had been sung centuries before, unbroken in their connection to the past. I was experiencing something profoundly rare that was disappearing. There are so many similarities to my time with the nightingales. Every night I left the field, it felt as though I could be saying farewell to another friend and song companion, so gifted and steeped in the essence of the land.

At the end of 2018 I realised that my work as a song collector was coming to an inevitable end. I was spending weeks on end pinballing across Ireland mostly, knocking on the doors of old people, to be told too often that I was 'months too late – if only you'd come sooner, poor Mary, God rest her soul, had all the old songs'. It was bleak work, and I often found myself reduced and haunted by ever-present death and loss, and not always loss of the old ones, either.

I became a father in 2018, just as the climate emergency response escalated. My calling to act as a protector was shifting. Extinction Rebellion (XR) arrived that September, and I found a tribe of fellow defenders dealing head-on with the biggest social and nature-concerned issue of our lifetime. My work in caravans on the sides of roads had now moved to barricades in the centre of the street, and a different fire in my belly had been sparked.

This was not a conscious closure, more a drifting – the acceptance of which didn't land properly until a chance encounter more than a year later. I had spent most of the week on the streets of London with the XR October uprising. I was cycling back into central London to hear Culture Declares run its 'Writers Rebel' event, with Robert Macfarlane, Ali Smith, Simon Schama, Simon McBurney and many other great writers speaking about their love of nature and fear of what is to come.

As I rode through Clerkenwell I was broadsided by an unexpectedly forceful gust of wind. I turned my handlebars to take the impact and was blown off-course down a street that I wasn't supposed to be on. But the spirit of jeopardy had been captain during those rebellious days, so I didn't resist and accepted my new course. Cycling onwards in the half-light of the evening, I found myself approaching Great Ormond Street Hospital. Opposite was a row of beautiful old Georgian houses. Through the darkness, one magnificent house stood out, with a bright, golden glow shining from its windows. I recognised it as a classical-music safe house. I stopped my bike to take a photograph and, as I did so, a lilting voice behind me caught my ears. The street was busy with patients' families having cigarettes breaks and taking the air, and just beside me was a group of about six smartly dressed men in their forties and fifties, whose voices I recognised instantly as those of Irish Travellers.

'Why's you taking a photo?' one of them asked.

'Hi,' I said. 'Isn't it beautiful, and it's even got a piano', which was playing as we spoke.

In thick, goading Irish he immediately retorted, 'D'yous want a piano? I'll sell you a piano.'

I got chatting and asked where they were from. 'Ach, we're not talking about that.' Travellers usually avoid revealing anything about themselves, if a complete stranger asks personal questions.

So I said, 'Are you McDonaghs or are you Joyces?' These are the two main Irish Traveller families in the Home Counties that I know and have collected songs and stories from.

Surprised, the eldest answered, 'We're Joyces. How do you know?'

Hopeful that I was guessing the correct member of the family, I replied 'I know your father, Christie Joyce.' He's a well-known patriarch and one of last of the tinsmiths who had the old ways with metalwork, and lives on a site outside Oxford.

'Jeez, how d'ye know old Christy?'

I explained that I'd been out to his site and recorded him. The Travellers were completely bemused by this, and when I told them that I sing the old songs, they at once urged me to sing. I obliged with a song that I had heard another Joyce family member sing back in Ireland, and before I could get to the end of the second line, one of them cut across me with, 'Ach. Gee, I hate dat old song.'

Given the location, I guessed they were probably taking a breather from an awful situation with a sick child, so I didn't want to intrude too much. To show I cared, I asked after an older couple who also shared the site: Ellie and John Mungins, who sang some of the oldest songs there are, some astoundingly ancient ballads. John had the rare gift of telling tales, too: headless-horseman stories, the ancient 'Jack tales' – tales that go back basically thousands of years, way beyond British shores. I had only managed to half-record them twice, never managing to get back to them when they were ready, or in good enough health, to go deep into their knowledge. But how many times I had pulled off the A40 to try.

'Ach, both of them dead this year' was the reply.

Hearing this news came like a punch to the stomach: that this sweet, hard-lived couple had left us, and with them a prolific legacy had gone undocumented, and they had never received the recognition and value they deserved. In that moment the reality of the time we live in hit home. As I cycled off from the hospital, I realised that what I'd done for the past decade and a half – collecting the old lore from these wisdom-keepers, these 'endlings' – that time was almost over. The old proverb of the house being on fire came to mind. There I was in some small room, trying to rescue some stunning gems from a little cupboard, when actually I needed to join the firefighters and confront the bigger issue that we all face now.

We live in an age of extinction, and of these same conditions affecting our fragile cultural ecosystems; and their equivalent is also threatening the nightingales and millions of other species – habitat change and loss, the pressures of dominant monocultures / monocrops, underfunding / underfeeding, and so on. I am motivated by the same urge to identify the last survivors of a bird community, fast losing their song in this country, and to acknowledge and gift our appreciation. Paying that respect, being present and pausing to give renewed adoration towards that small, quiet beauty, so hidden from our daily worlds: this is the most powerful and vital act we can make to reconnect and bring re-enchantment back to the natural world and into our lives.

Are these not times in which we need to take every opportunity to fill our hearts with the richness our land offers? As nature connectivity vanishes, so we have a national dearth in traditions of guidance and stewardship to bring our young people to nature appreciation, although there are many inspirational projects, campaigns, campaigners, writers and artists working to reverse that trend. Today, we adults have such a reduced degree of the confidence we once had to go and seek out the wonderment and well-being that nature bestows. A few hours in the serenity of the dark, the indiscrimination of the night and the clandestine childlikeness of being so outrageous as to step beyond the known realm always create a profound experience.

Add a nightingale to that cocktail and you have Mother Nature's most powerful tonic, with the added privilege of it being drunk from the cup of her very own hands.

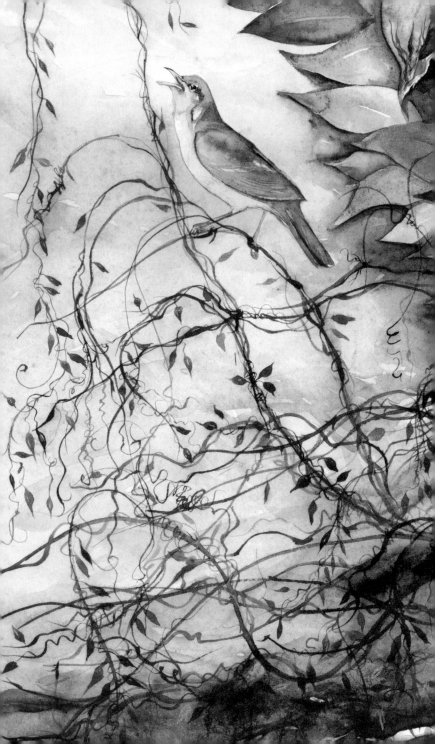

BIBLIOGRAPHY

Reading list

Edward A. Armstrong, *The Folklore of Birds* [facsimile edition] (William Collins, 2009)

Mark Cocker and Richard Maybe, *Birds Britannica* (Chatto & Windus, 2005)

Mark Cocker and David Tipling, *Birds & People* (Jonathan Cape, 2013)

Bob Cooper, *A Song for Every Season* (William Heinemann, 1971)

Francesca Greenoak, *All the Birds of the Air: The names, lore and literature of British birds* (Deutsch, 1979)

Beatrice Harrison [ed. Patricia Cleveland-Peck], *The Cello and the Nightingales* (Hodder & Stoughton, 1985)

Ludwig Koch, *Memoirs of a Birdman* (Phoenix House, 1955)

Richard Mabey, *The Perfumer and The Stinkhorn: Six personal essays on natural science and Romanticism* (Profile Books, 2011)

Michael McCarthy, *Say Goodbye to the Cuckoo* (John Murray, 2009)

George Monbiot, *Feral: Searching for enlightenment on the frontiers of rewilding* (Allen Lane, 2013)

Jeremy Mynott, *Birds in the Ancient World* (Oxford University Press, 2018)

Jeremy Mynott, *Birdscapes: Birds in our imagination and experience* (Princeton University Press, 2009)

Alex Preston and Neil Gower, *As Kingfishers Catch Fire: Birds & Books* (Corsair, 2017)

David Rothenberg, *Why Birds Sing: A journey into the mystery of birdsong* (Basic Books, 2005)

David Rothenberg, *Nightingales in Berlin: Searching for the perfect sound* (University of Chicago Press, 2019)

Adrian Thomas, *RSPB Guide to Birdsong* (Bloomsbury Wildlife, 2019)

Mike Toms, *Flight Lines: Tracking the wonders of bird migration* (BTO, 2017)

Isabella Tree, *Wilding: The Return of Nature to a British Farm* (Picador, 2018)

Gilbert White, *The Natural History of Selborne* [facsimile edition] (Oxford University Press, 2013)

Jon Young, Evan McGown et al, *Coyote's Guide to Connecting with Nature* (Owlink Media, 2010)

Resources

Birdlife International: www.birdlife.org

British Trust for Ornithology: www.bto.org

RSPB: www.rspb.org.uk

Singing with Nightingales: www.singingwithnightingales.com

The Wildlife Trusts: www.wildlifetrusts.org

The Woodland Trust: www.woodlandtrust.org.uk

ACKNOWLEDGEMENTS

My thanks go to all those who have guided me to the nightingale and helped deepen my understanding and expand the bird's mystery. Special thanks to Becky Burchell, Nick Lear, Rachel Millward, New Networks for Nature, the Renton Family, David Rothenberg, Tom Stuart for his exceptional knowledge and brilliant ears, the RSPB's Adrian Thomas, and Tiff Wear. Thanks also to the British Trust for Ornithology, Royal Society for the Protection of Birds and BirdLife International. But my most special thanks go to Oran Summer, my daughter, who when first taken to find nightingales aged three months, managed to entice a male bird to sing above us in full sight – something I never imagined I'd witness.

Thanks to those who have dared to join my reckless journeys in the dark, torch-free, and shown how important the nightingale's song is for us hear and protect. Very special thanks to my editor Zennor Compton for her stern, compassionate guidance of this wayward troubadour to learn to stay home and write, and for trusting in a dyslexic itinerant that a book was in there somewhere. Also to my manager and guide Paul Burger for all his hard work here too. Massive thank you to Jess Barnfield, Rachel Campbell, Sasha Cox, Konrad Kirkham, Roy McMillan, Kasim Mohammed, Sam Rees-Williams, Katie Sheldrake, Claire Simmonds, Joanna Taylor, Mat Watterson, Klara Zak and the wonderful team at Penguin Random House for your commitment and patience!

Thanks also to: Simon Armitage, Thom Ashworth, Amy-Jane Beer, Pam Bedard, Jessica Blackstone, Nathalie Blue, Charlie Brotherstone, Joseph Browning, Nathalie Caldini, Dora Cloutick, Lily Cole, Sophie Cowan, Culture Declares Emergency, Sarah Darwin, Ollie Denton, Mike Drew, Sarah Dudney, Mauro Durante, Extinction Rebellion, Piers Faccini, John Fanshawe, Shehani Fernando, Ed Gillespie, Malcolm Green, Martin Harper, Jo Hindley, Tiana Jacout, Rose Jamieson and all at The Nest Collective, Kerenyi Zsuzsanna Kerenyi, Chris King, Kate Latham, Devon Léger, Martin and MaryAnn at Greenfarm, Luke Massey, Julian May, Sara Mohr-Pietsch, Music Declares Emergency, Lucy Neal, Max O'Brien, Vladimír Potančok, Bethan Roberts, Laurence Rose, Cosmo Sheldrake, Harriet Simms, Tristram Stuart, Mike Toms, Isabella Tree, Araceli Tzigane, Lucie Uhlíková, Jarmila Vlčková, Marija Vitas, Vron Ware, Caroline Whitman and Georgia Ruth Williams.

LIST OF IMAGES
In order of appearance

J. A. Naumann's Naturgeschichte der Vögel, Naumann, Johann Andreas © The British Library Board

Robin. Familiar Wild Birds by W Swaysland (Cassell, c 1900) c Look and Learn/Bridgeman Images/Redstart. Familiar Wild Birds by W Swaysland (Cassell, c 1900) c Look and Learn/Bridgeman Images/Svenska Faglar efter Naturen och pa sten ritade. By Magnus, Wilhelm and Ferdinand von Wright c Purix Verlag Volker Christen/Bridgeman Images

The Nightingale's migration route © Darren Bennett/DKB Creative

Rostock Pfeilstorch, Zoologische Sammlung der Universität Rostock | © Wikipedia

Nightingale distribution in the UK © Darren Bennett/DKB Creative

Thrush nightingale, Luscinia luscinia © Mary Evans Picture Library

NIGHTINGALE SINGING © Mary Evans Picture Library

Just a Song at Sunset... (Luscinia megarhyncus) © Mary Evans Picture Library

Nightingale Song, Topical Press Agency/Stringer © Getty Images

For The Birds, Topical Press Agency/Stringer © Getty Images

Nightingale © Look and Learn/Bridgeman Images

North east view of Selbourne © British Library Board. All Rights Reserved/Bridgeman Images

Eugenio Bettoni, Storia naturale degli uccelli che nidificano in Lombardia DE AGOSTINI PICTURE LIBRARY/Contributor | © Getty Images

Antique illustration of nightingales (Luscinia megarhynchos) and nest – stock illustration, illbusca | © Getty Images

THE NIGHTINGALE

'Jack-in-the-Green', a May-Day Scene Sixty Years ago (engraving), Look and Learn/
Illustrated Papers Collection/Bridgeman Images

Nightingale, nest and egg, Luscinia megarhynchos © Mary Evans Picture Library

Nightingale © Look and Learn/Bridgeman Images

Luscinia megarhynchos, common nightingale © Mary Evans Picture Library

1 kuna coin, 1993, obverse, nightingale, Croatia, 20th century © A. Dagli Orti/De
Agostini Picture Library/Bridgeman Images

Nightingale, benoitb © Getty Images

The Nightingale of France, c.1830 (colour litho) © Archives Charmet/Bridgeman
Images

Philomele and Progne – Philomel And Progne © Bridgeman Images

– Nightingale, Luscinia megarhynchos © Mary Evans Picture Library

Nightingale Illustration Andrew_Howe © Getty Images

Nightingales singing at night, clu © Getty Images

The Emperor and the Nightingale, illustration for 'The Nightingale' from *Fairy
Tales* by Hans Christian Andersen © Archives Charmet/Bridgeman Images

The Hawk and the Nightingale, from *A Hundred Fables of Aesop*, 1903 (engraving) ©
The Stapleton Collection/Bridgeman Images

Philomel and Progne from *Fontaine Fables*, pub. 1905 (engraving) © The Stapleton
Collection/Bridgeman Images

Roses and Nightingale, late 18th century (ink & colour on paper) © Gift of Nasrin
and Abolala Soudavar/Bridgeman Images

Samuel Taylor Coleridge, Culture Club/Contributor © Getty Images/John Keats,
English poet, and his Ode to a Nightingale, 1819 (1958), Print Collector/Contribu-
tor © Getty Images/John Clare, Edward Gooch Collection/Stringer © Getty

Nightingale and the Bomber, © ATM

Nightingale's Nest (engraving) © Look and Learn/Bridgeman Images

Nightingale on its nest © Mary Evans Picture Library

Natural History, Nightingale (Luscinia megarhynchos), duncan1890 © Getty
Images

Nightingale and Oak, © Angela Harding

The Bear and Nightingales © Jackie Morris